GEMS OF LOVE

To pray is to direct one's mind, heart, soul and spirit towards the Source of Life from which we have emerged. Prayer is a connection and communion with God.

Praying is tuning the consciousness to the higher worlds. Such tuning is similar to tuning the strings of a violin.

I pray with all my heart that God may enlighten you and bless you more and more abundantly, so that you may be filled with that Divine Spirit, with its vast and inexhaustible Love.

Beinsa Douno

Photograph by Wajko Iskrenoff
The Master speaks on the basic nature of prayer to his disciples in front of the prayer hall of the Brotherhood of Light in the Isgrev quarter of Sofia.

Gems of Love

Prayers and Formulas

BEINSA DOUNO
(Peter Deunov)

Translated from the Bulgarian
by
David Lorimer

For Phyllida

with my blessing

[signature]

September 2023

The Grain of Wheat Trust

Published by The Grain of Wheat Trust
Copyright © The Grain of Wheat Trust 1994
The Universal Brotherhood of Light
ISBN 0 9522862 0 3

The Grain of Wheat

Any reader wishing further information about the work of Beinsa Douno should write to the Secretary, The Grain of Wheat, 258 Kew Road, Richmond, Surrey TW9 3EG.

Acknowledgements

Thanks are due to John Miller for his help in typesetting the book, and to Katilina Green for her assistance with translation.

Printed by Beshara Press Ltd., Cheltenham GL50 3LQ

CONTENTS

FOREWORD
by the Translator

The Master Beinsa Douno (Peter Deunov) was born in Bulgaria in 1864. He began intensive preparations for his teaching mission on his return from America in 1895, and inaugurated the Bulgarian Universal Brotherhood of Light in 1900. From then on he travelled the country, teaching and healing, until he settled in Sofia during the First World War. In 1914, he spent part of the summer in the small village of Arbanassi. It was there, on a mountain peak nearby, that Christ appeared to him and said:

Give me your body, your heart and your mind and work for me.

The Master answered:

Lord, may your will be done. I am ready.

It was in that same year that he began teaching more systematically. Over the next thirty years he gave some 7,000 lectures and talks, which are collected in over 150 volumes in Bulgarian. Since the revolution of 1989, publishing has been resumed, with old books being reprinted as well as unpublished material appearing for the first time. By the time of his death in 1944, Beinsa Douno had some 40,000 followers in Bulgaria.

Beinsa Douno is the greatest spiritual figure to appear in Bulgaria since the time of the Bogomils and St. John of Rila in the tenth century. Of divine revelations he said: 'The One who speaks down the centuries is always the Same. At all times it is God who reveals Himself to humanity. The forms through which He manifests are different, but He is One'.

In describing his own mission he says:

> *I am a messenger from the Divine World, sent to proclaim Love and to bring its strength and power into life. Every Divine Teacher is invulnerable. Divine Knowledge is eternal, indivisible: it was so in the past, it is so in the present, it will be so in the future. As a result, the person who has taught it, who teaches it, who will teach it, does not count. It is always the Spirit of God that counts, in all times and in all ages, and no worldly power can overcome it.*
>
> *I have not come of my own wish, but God has sent me to work for the restoration of His Kingdom on earth. God spoke through Christ. God is speaking through me.*
>
> *The ideas I am giving in the talks and lectures are taken from the Divine. What Christ said and what I am saying come from one and the same source. There are no two sources.*
>
> *I have come to manifest Love and bring it to earth. This is my mission.*
>
> *The truths are hidden in the lectures. I have deposited these truths there for future generations.*
>
> *I am turning to you: I am the Door. The Door is Love.*

From the foregoing it can be seen that Beinsa Douno stresses the continuity of his mission with that of Christ. This is also apparent in the key principles of his Teaching, which are Love, Wisdom and Truth:

> *The first principle on which the whole of existence is based is Love; it brings the impulse to life; it is the compass, the stimulus within the human soul.*
>
> *The second principle is Wisdom, which brings knowledge and light to the mind, thus enabling human beings to use the forces of Nature in a noetic way.*

The third principle is Truth: it frees the human soul from bondage and encourages her to learn, to work well and make efforts towards self-sacrifice.

There is nothing greater than these three principles; there is no straighter or surer path. In these principles lies the salvation of the world!

He urges us to apply:

The Living fire of Love,
The Living Light of Wisdom,
The Living power of Truth.
Love out of which life springs is true Love,
Wisdom out of which light emanates is true Wisdom,
Truth whence freedom comes is Truth indeed.
The Spirit reigns therein.
God is light in which the fruits of Virtue ripen.
Great ideas dwell in noble souls,
Radiant and brilliant thoughts in radiant and brilliant minds,
Pure desires in pure hearts.
We shall speak forth to the diligent disciples
With the beaming rays of light,
In the presence of Love, Wisdom and Truth.
May Love, Wisdom and Truth abide with you,
Now and throughout eternity.
May they sustain and illumine
All that is good and sublime within you.
These are the words of life.
Blessed are those who walk in Wisdom,
For they shall abide in the Light.
Blessed are those who live in the Truth,
For they shall be freed from the chains of all limitations.
This is the Eternal Testament of the Spirit.

A key feature of the spiritual practice of Beinsa Douno is connection with Nature. A number of physical exercises are accompanied by the recital of formulas, while the sacred movements of the paneurythmy express an exchange of energy between human beings and the intelligent forces of the natural world. Even now, the main gathering of the Brotherhood in Bulgaria is a summer camp in the Rila Mountains. The mountains are the real context of these prayers. They are said at sunrise and again at sunset, interspersed with some of the beautiful songs also composed by the Master and played by the disciples on the violin and other instruments. The spiritual practice has three expressions: in music, movement and prayer. There is thus an integration between the spiritual, physical, ecological and musical dimensions.

A word should be said about the style and presentation of these prayers. It is only in the last decade or so that there has been widespread awareness of masculine bias in religious and spiritual expressions and vocabulary. In his lectures, Beinsa Douno uses the word *chovek* for human being, which I have translated as person; I have generally rephrased the pronouns to express them in the plural, thus avoiding the tendentious use of 'he'. A similar problem occurs with the use of 'He' for God. Here I have kept to the original usage, but it should not be interpreted as meaning that Beinsa Douno regarded God as only possessing masculine attributes. After a good deal of thought, I have also decided to retain the now archaic 'Thou' and 'Thee' forms of address. I am no enthusiast for modern versions which desacralise the language, as so often happens in new translations. I am also aware that all other European languages, including Bulgarian, retain the distinction between second person singular and second person plural forms of address. It seems to me that the sacred resonance of the prayers is better expressed in this form.

D.L. October 1993.

References:

Prophet for Our Times, edited by David Lorimer (Element Books, 1991)

The Circle of Sacred Dance, edited by David Lorimer (Element Books, 1991)

INTRODUCTION

Prayers made with love are always received

Without prayer a person cannot make progress. Christ himself prayed every night. He had a great deal of knowledge, but he prayed every night. As if he needed to pray! ...Why must we pray? The Apostle Paul says: 'Be constant in prayer' and Christ teaches: 'Watch and pray!' There is no record of person dying while praying! The Scriptures say: 'The Angel of the Lord protects those who pray and trust in God'

You should pray unceasingly, you should be grateful for everything, you should always rejoice, because that is the Will of God for you in Jesus Christ.

'Do not extinguish the Spirit!', said St. Paul.

People must pray if they want to learn! Pray to be liberated from all impurities which tarnish you! Every living creature prays! Prayer is a conscious process of the human soul!

Prayer has a threefold character. It is equivalent to breathing. People should pray as a means for the soul to breathe in order to assimilate things. Prayer is essential to the soul. It is the contemplation of the most sublime feelings. With prayer we see the child praying, it is a call; just as breathing is necessary for the body, so is prayer necessary for the soul. People need air more than food. It has been proved that people can hold their breath for a maximum of 25 minutes. If we equate air with prayer, which is the food of the soul, we appreciate its enormous importance.

Prayer is a Divine impulse. Therefore it is said that we

1

should pray in every circumstance because it has an influence on all spheres of life. Later on you can all try an experiment as find out how many of your prayers God has answered. However, when you pray, do not tell anyone why you pray and what you expect from it until the results are obvious and have happened, because, if you tell anyone, it is quite possible to hinder yourself and so you yourself will be to blame.

Prayer has the power to heal any infirmities and illnesses. It is a means of being able to cure disease. All our work will be successful if you begin the work with prayer. Whoever perseveres in prayer will see and confirm that the Lord is true; but you must persist in prayer until such time that you lose the urge to pray, which shows that your prayer has been answered positively or negatively. But prayer should express our gratitude for all the good things and blessings which God is giving us.

The best exercise in human life is prayer. At present there is no better exercise in the world than prayer. Prayer is one of the best methods of purifying the mind and the feelings.

And so remember the following Truth: 'There is no greater thing in life than prayer'. Whatever else people say to you, don't forget the meaning and necessity of prayer and communion with God. No knowledge, no Love, no Wisdom in the world could compare with prayer, with a person's communion with the Primary Principle.

There is no greater moment than when one directs one's eyes and heart upwards towards the One, who has given you everything. If you continue working in this way throughout the year, you will always be joyful and happy and you will feel the presence of God. In all circumstances, prayer will have the power to help! You always need to pray!

What is Prayer?

Prayer is communion with God, a link with the Great origin of life. If our prayer does not link us with God, what is the use of it? Prayer is a force. It enlivens and animates knowledge. It uplifts and inspires, giving strength to the mind, the heart, the soul and the spirit.

Prayer is a conversation of the soul with God. To pray means to send your report to that centre from which you have emerged. What are you going to write in the report? About the work which you have done. In reply to this you will receive peace and enlightenment.

Prayer is the bond between the human soul and God, by means of which people confess their mistakes, rectify themselves and give thanks for all the good things which they receive every day. Prayer is not a request for material goods, it helps us move towards the perfection of God, to become pure in heart, radiant in mind and loving like God.

Prayer is a sacred form of action which every person must perform at all times and which they must not postpone.

True prayer means the awakening of the consciousness and superconsciousness of people, i.e. the awakening of the Divine within them. In this way the power of God is transmitted to people, by means of which people forget low and worldly things, they rise higher than the ordinary and everyday.

Prayer is a deep inner process of the human soul. Prayer is work, a deep desire of the human soul to achieve something sublime. Prayer is the most powerful action in human life. It concentrates human thinking, human feeling and human will in a single whole. Such prayer is mighty, it accomplishes miracles.

Prayer is a process which governs the forces of good and evil. It is a free action of the human soul and spirit. If thinking, feeling and acting do not partake in prayer, this is not true prayer. Prayer is a Divine law which pervades the whole of existence.

Nourishment, singing and praying are the three introductions to conscious life. What is most necessary for human beings is nourishment, what is most pleasing is music and what is most powerful is prayer. Nourishment is an initiation to physical life, music is an initiation to spiritual life and prayer is an initiation to Divine life. Nourishment brings health, singing brings happiness and prayer brings bliss.

Prayer is the greatest and most powerful means of linking to God, to the eternal within us, which reveals the meaning of life. If you are in relationship with God, you will be resurrected.

Prayer is a conversation, a communion with God. Since the human soul contains the accumulation of the ages within itself, it cannot understand the Will of God. That is why one has to pray to God. God will purify you, will free you from that burden so that you can know yourself, know your neighbour and know God. Prayer is a method for resolving the most difficult tasks.

The soul needs inner spiritual food, which can only be supplied through prayer. Prayer has a magical strength!

Prayer must be conscious and have a definite aim. Children pray to their mother whom they know. Their prayer is exactly defined. They know what they want and who they want it from.

God loves short but meaningful prayers. Every word must be in its place. You must mention which errors you are praying for so that God will help you be free of them and so that you can develop the appropriate virtues. Open yourself to God, wish for His Light and Strength so that you do not repeat your mistakes.

Prayer should not be one-sided, only for your own benefit. Since it is an expression of the soul, we should request what our spirit desires.

How should one pray?

Prayer does not consist of the mechanical recital of words. People must come down from their exalted positions, humble themselves and pray like a child to God. And so, when you pray, the image of God must be present in your mind. No other image! You will say – we don't know what the image of God is like. On the contrary, you do know that image! Now you only have to bring it to mind!

I listen to how you read prayers – you are in a hurry to finish as quickly as possible. When I pray, the Good Prayer takes me fifteen minutes, the 91st psalm takes twenty minutes, the Path of Life takes twenty minutes and when I read Our Father, it takes half an hour, and when I get to the

Prayer of the Kingdom it takes another half hour. But if you are in a hurry, nothing will be achieved. Those fifteen minutes represent the law by means of which all misunderstandings are dispelled, twenty minutes is the law of creation and work, thirty minutes is the law of equilibrium. Whoever does not understand these laws will be discouraged, while whoever understands them will use the fifteen, twenty and thirty minutes in prayer and in reading the Bible.

How should you pray? When you get up in the morning, look at your forehead and say 'Lord, bless my forehead and the capacities which are hidden within. If your thinking is not right, stroke your nose and send your thoughts towards God. If your eyes are not seeing properly, stroke them. If you do not eat and speak properly, pray for and stroke your mouth. If you cannot hear properly, stroke your ears and pray for them. After that you will stroke your hands and feet, which serve you well. Be grateful for the faculties which have been given you to use.

When you pray, you should concentrate so that you can forget everything else around you. Your thought should be directed exclusively towards God. No other image! Then your prayer will be received. True prayer means turning deeply within yourself, isolating yourself; nobody should see you, you should forget everything else. People can isolate themselves even when they are in company. This solitude is not an outer process. When praying, you will enter your secret chamber. Pray secretly within your soul.

Prayer does not only entail the lighting of icon-lamps, prostration, but it consists of participation in the life of your neighbours. If you meet a hungry person, feed them, if you meet a person with torn clothes, dress them. There is no better prayer than this.

It is stated simply and clearly: 'Enter into your secret chamber where no human feet have trodden. Only angels live there. And when you go inside, pray to your Father, who sees in secret. When you enter this chamber, you will understand what God is! What does this secret prayer mean? It means closing the telephone lines linked with the outside world. When a person is praying within themselves, they have to be free; they should disconnect every line with the world; they should be deaf to every noise and every sound from within and without.

The best posture for praying is for a person to be upright. You will stand upright and not look upwards but straight ahead (perpendicular to your forehead). When praying you will look straight ahead. When you organise a time for prayer, God will be in front of you. David says 'I could see God in front of my face'. As soon as God is in front of your face, you will know that He sees everything, recognises all your needs and is able to help you.

When you read a prayer, read it slowly, calmly and thoughtfully – so that you remain content with this action. When people pray, they should pronounce it exactly and definitely, they should express their thought succinctly and not pray for themselves but for everyone and for the common good. Pray for everybody, even for your enemies.

How will you know that you have received an answer to your prayer? By that quiet inner joy, by that inner light, which will help you in resolving various questions. Some people receive an instant answer to their prayers, while others wait days, months or even years. It depends on the strength of the prayer.

Sometimes you will see that prayer does not work – you pray and receive no answer. In this case you resemble a person who wants to lift an enormous weight, but is not able to because it is beyond his strength. Then he asks others to come and help him – together they can achieve it. Sometimes you will need the help of one, two, three or more people. Therefore, if we do not succeed in our prayer, we will seek the help of one, two or three brothers or sisters, depending on the need, until we prevail. Try this out, and you will see the extent to which this can be applied in practice.

Until you live through something really dreadful, your prayer will be superficial and goes no deeper. When you encounter great suffering, you send out a deep and burning prayer towards God, which is transmitted directly into the invisible world.

If your mind is disturbed, ask God for help. If your heart craves for something, pray to God for a successful outcome. Pray for everything, and reveal it all to God. Contemporary people expect great results, even though they do not fulfil the Will of their Great Father. That is impossible. God listens to and answers only those who are born of the Spirit.

Whoever prays from the bottom of their heart will invariably receive an answer! If you are working towards the realignment of your life, God will listen to you and answer your prayer. There isn't a living being in the world – small or large – whose appeal God has not responded to. There are no instances when God has not responded to any living soul.

When to pray

The Scripture says: 'Pray without ceasing, and give thanks for everything!'. You can pray even when you are walking around. You can get up, fall down, and still go on praying. Whoever lives according to the laws of Love will always be disposed to pray. In the life of a loving person, everything is a prayer. Whatever the circumstances, maintain your connection with the Great Centre of Life and do not be afraid. Always pray and offer everything to God. When a person thinks about God, they are protected. Wherever you go and whatever work you begin, you need energy. If you give yourself over to the outside world, the world will force you off the path of you life.

Christ spent hours in prayer after midnight. Why? During these hours he was filled with energy like a dynamo. He then used that energy during the day. In other words, we draw energy from God while praying. The most favourable hours for prayer are the early hours after midnight – one, three and five o'clock. You should pray both when you are well and when you are unwell. Even when you are scorned by everybody, raise your eyes towards God with these words: 'God bless these people!' That is real Love towards God.

Every one of you who wants to be a disciple must choose a sacred hour for work. Spend this hour in deep meditation. You should observe this sacred hour throughout the year and work towards the restoration of harmony in your relations, towards the overcoming of difficulties and towards your spiritual elevation.

When the impulse to pray comes to you, you should not

delay, but enter the secret chamber of your heart and pray, and that prayer will be accepted. If you delay, it is possible that the spirit will not come to dispose you towards prayer again. Therefore we can pray at any time. When we are among bad people, we should pray for patience, so that a fortress is formed around you which is inaccessible to bad influences – if they have attacked your soul, they can be expelled. The person who does not pray severs their link with God and evil invades them.

People need the light of God. People pray best when they are persecuted, when they are undergoing the greatest suffering and hardship. Such prayer is stronger and more intense.

UNION WITH GOD

*A lecture given by the Master on 23rd November 1930
at Izgrev, Sofia.*

In its manifestations, life has a real side and an unreal side. These manifestations have both a practical and theoretical significance. For example: a person's belief is one of the theoretical sides of life. What they think about faith is still theory. In such a case, all people have different theoretical conceptions about belief and life. However, in relation to the real side of life, people in general – like all living beings – arrive at the same conceptions and have the same experiences. Thus there is unity in the reality of things. For instance, when joy comes it creates the same conditions and changes in all living beings. It is in human beings that these changes are most evident. When they are glad, their pulse becomes quicker, the flow of blood into the heart increases and all organs expand. In general, joy brings about an expansion in human beings.

Another real side of life is prayer. The person who does not know how to pray is only theorising. However, to theorise about prayer cannot be called real prayer. People today think that prayer is only appropriate for simple people. They think that prayer is a humiliating thing for the scholar or genius. However, in actual fact, if one studies the lives of geniuses or scholars, one realises that it is a prayer from beginning to end. Their life begins with prayer and ends with prayer. The prayer of the genius, for instance, shows that he is buzzing with some sublime idea, thanks to which he wishes to bring something to the world. Such a

11

life is completely altruistic. Hence we say that the genius – like the saint – is not seeking any personal interest in their life.

Thus everyone who is prepared to understand prayer in an inward, intuitive fashion is able to grasp the deep meaning of prayer. In contemporary languages one does not find words to express the great idea hidden in the word 'prayer'. For want of an exact definition in different languages, one uses approximate words. To pray means to direct one's mind, one's heart, one's soul and one's spirit towards that Source of Life from which we have emerged. If people are becoming rough, it is because they rarely remember the Primordial Principle of life. Therefore the decadence of present day humanity is due to a profound inner cause: the neglect of the Primordial Principle from which it sprang. Contemporary people neglect God. One often hears it said: 'I am a free person, I can do without God, I have no need to pray'.

This is the reasoning of the person who thinks themselves free, but this reasoning is not logically correct. Why? For the sole reason that the real and absolute in the world is indivisible. The One who has created us cannot forget us; nor do we have the right to forget Him. Were He to forget us, we would be finished: it would be death. And if we forget Him, the same fate awaits us. You say: Why would we die? I will show you why death would come. To ask if one can live without prayer is equivalent to asking if one can live without breathing. If a person thinks that they are independent and free, they should try to stop breathing, even if only for an hour. People will spontaneously understand the necessity of breathing if they try not to breathe for an hour. If breathing is so essential to human beings, thinking of God is a thousand times more indispensable. The more a person remembers God and maintains this thought within themselves, the nobler they are. The nobility of the human soul depends on its thought about God. Hence, if we wish to be noble, we must remember God as the Essence of Life which passes through us. In all conditions of life, in joy and in sorrow, we must think of God. Apart from God no education, no nobility, no science, religion, arts and crafts have any existence.

It is said that culture can exist without God. I say: just as life on earth cannot exist without the sun, no culture can exist without God. Just as vegetation cannot exist without water, nor human beings without air, culture cannot exist without God. By means of these analogies I wish to show the great necessity of prayer. Human thought cannot develop without prayer. We are not referring here to corrupted forms of human thought, according to which the idea of God is represented as a caricature. Contemporary ideas about God are those of a culture in decline. Everything they think of as real is in fact unreal.

How many times people have prayed to God and not received a response! Why? Praying to God and not receiving a response can be compared with the state of person parched with thirst – dreaming that they are drinking water – and who, on waking up, is still thirsty. Is the water they drink in the dream real? Reality is defined by the fact that it can satisfy every inner feeling which has distressed people. In reality people grow continuously.

In this evening's meeting I would like you to understand the reality of prayer and how to pray. I would like to hear from one of you how to pray. When you pray, that is, when you go to God, you are embarrassed. If you are embarrassed, can you pray properly? Why are you uneasy? When pupils have learned their lesson properly, they get up quickly and courageously, and respond with ease to all the questions posed by the teacher. If, however, they have not studied their lesson, they feel awkward and think: The teacher will fail me. When you pray to God, you should think of his qualities: God is infinitely patient, but also very demanding. When people pray, they should do so for real and necessary things. God does not like us to pray for useless things. We must not expect God to do things which we can do for ourselves. It is ridiculous to pray God: 'Lord, teach me how to eat!... Teach me to drink!... How to shake hands with people!... to dress!... etc. Many prayers by people today are of this kind.

I say: people nowadays need the kind of prayer which can improve their lives and remove greed. Greed is a vice, a wound which is eating away at the human soul. Greed darkens human consciousness and hardens the heart. Greedy people think only of themselves all day long. They want to eat well, be well dressed, have a warm and comfortable home, be in good health etc. The sufferings of other people do not interest them. They say: 'That is not my concern'. Neglecting one's neighbour is an alien influence on human beings. This condition is rarely imposed on them, but it has such a nasty smell that people will have to purify themselves for a long time afterwards in order to be free of it.

So remember the following truth: there is nothing more noble in human life than prayer. Despite everything anyone can say to the contrary, *never forget the importance, the absolute necessity of prayer, of union with God. Neither knowledge, nor Love, nor Wisdom on earth are in any way comparable with what prayer brings about: union with the Primordial Principle.*

The power of prayer lies in this: when a person prays, they activate all their virtues. Prayer in which all the virtues are not activated cannot be considered genuine. Prayer must simultaneously contain the qualities of Love, Wisdom, Truth, Justice, Compassion and many other virtues. If you go to God with a prayer of this kind, you will resemble a tree laden with ripe fruit. When God sees you adorned in this way, He will be glad to have an intelligent child near Him – one who knows how to speak such a sublime, angelic language.

You think: 'We cannot all be such intelligent and noetic children!' That doesn't matter. God tolerates ignorant children as well. However, the stupid child can never achieve the same results as the intelligent one. This difference is evident everywhere in life. The intelligent one learns, while the stupid one is always putting things off; the intelligent one is rewarded, the stupid one consoled.

I say: if contemporary people did not know how to pray, they would already have lost the little that they have kept until now. All the beautiful, all the great, all the good that they have preserved is thanks to the spirit of prayer which is working in their soul. It is thanks to prayer – even though it is not properly done, such as it is practised today – that people have retained within themselves something beautiful and acquire something new. It is thanks to prayer that we become conductors of higher Powers and beneficial means by which the whole human race is sustained. The soul needs an inner spiritual food which can only be provided through prayer.

Now, in observing you, I notice the following thing: you are enriched by the knowledge which I give you; but you have not yet learned how to pray. Often, you think as I think, you philosophise like me, you speak like I speak, you preach like I do; but you do not pray like I pray. Praying is the only thing which I cannot teach you. I never allow myself to teach anyone how they must pray. Why? According to me, prayer is the most sacred action – the sole prerogative of the soul.

People ask me: 'How do you pray and when do you pray? I cannot tell you how I pray, but I am always praying; I am praying when I eat, when I drink water, when I read and when I work. I am praying everywhere and all the time. 'Isn't it hard to pray so much?' No, on the contrary. It makes me lighter. The meaning of life is in fact to be found in prayer. When a person stops praying, life disappears. Prayer is a sublime thing which is not expressed by a mechanical recital. When you have learned to pray, your life will acquire its meaning. The disciples of Christ didn't know how to pray either. They turned to Him and asked: 'Master, teach us to pray'. And Christ replied: 'When the Spirit of Truth comes, He will teach you'. But in the face of Christ they had an image of genuine prayer.

I say: Every person can learn to pray. If prayer depends on a person's virtues, they must make goodness the basis of their life. If they manage to establish this basis, their capacity for prayer will develop without their noticing it – like a natural result of life. Then the soul of that person will be like a tree with thousands of sweet smelling flowers. When people are in a state to pray, evil does not exist for them, and they are well disposed towards everyone. They rejoice in everything and are grateful for everything. On seeing a little worm in difficulties, such a person will stop and try to help it in some way. If they look at a tree whose branches are being tormented by the wind, they feel a tender compassion for it and the desire to be of some help. Everything springs to life before such people. They see the Spirit of God manifesting everywhere, working and helping. This awakens an inner impulse to work as well and to achieve liberation from the limited conditions of life.

You ask: 'Is it only human beings who pray?' Every living creature prays. Animals and plants also pray. The scents which plants spread in the air are their prayer. When the plant loses its scent, it dries up. So long as it retains its scent, it grows and develops. As a result, people emit a pleasant scent, like a flower, when they are praying. The more they pray, the more intense their scent becomes. When they stop praying, their scent gradually diminishes. The person who has never prayed or who has forgotten to pray gives out an unpleasant smell. Just as the quality of the plant determines the scent it gives out, so one can know a person's virtues in the same way. The more a person's virtues are developed, the further their scent extends.

Thus prayer is the most important work in life. The way one prays is an individual thing – which everyone must learn for themselves. If I were to show you how to pray, you would only hear an echo of the prayer, an echo which, in the long run, would not be appealing, and the desire to pray would leave you. Prayer has a meaning only when it emerges from the depths of the soul. If you want someone to show you how you should pray, they will say to you: 'I will pray for you; you will work for me'. Such is the law. If you work for someone, they must then pray for you. If they do not pray for you, you do not need to work for them. Such are the relationships between spiritual people. If, again, you pray for someone, they should work for you.

This evening I would like you to pray, then I will work; or else I will pray and you will work. Or else we can divide: one half will work and the other half will pray. Whatever you receive, it is important that you direct your thought towards God. There is no more sublime moment than when you raise your mind and heart towards the One who has given us everything. If you constantly work in this way throughout the year, your heart will continuously be full of joy and you will feel the presence of God. This prayer will have the power to help you in all the events of life.

Knowledge without prayer is tedious to people; religion without prayer is tedious to people; love without prayer is tedious to people; food without prayer is tedious to people. Everything which is done without prayer is difficult for the human spirit. There are people who are extremely pretentious in the prayers; their prayer is severe, measured and restrained. But there are people – particularly among the poor – from whom prayer springs freely and directly, such as they feel it in the moment. After such a prayer, the face of these people is lit up and smiling, while a certain change comes about in their soul.

Sometimes the poor pray in this way: 'Lord, there is something within me which wants to pray, but I don't know how to pray. I am sorry for the worries and time which I cause You in not yet knowing how to pray. I try to accomplish Your will, but I do not succeed: I carry on making errors. If You were to strike me, Your hand would crush me. Have mercy upon me, I will not repeat these same mistakes'. God, on hearing this prayer, sends His Blessing to that soul and says: 'That child is intelligent: he will put things right'.

I am explaining things in a human way – such as they happen among people. Who has not met in their life someone with a pure and sincere heart who speaks from the depth of their soul? When you hear such a person speak, you feel that they are ready to render any kind of service or make any kind of sacrifice on your behalf, so that you feel well disposed towards this person and are ready to forgive them any wrong they may do to you. I say: if you do not forgive the faults of those close to you, your own faults will not be forgiven. You often turn towards God in your prayer and ask to understand some mystery. You will learn many things, but only when you have learned to pray properly.

Observing you this evening, I see young and old among you. You all say that you love one another, that you have brotherly and sisterly relations. What differentiates the old and the young? The old person is distinguished by their concern to be of service to the younger brothers and sisters, and the young people are distinguished by their willingness to work. So both old and young are ready to accomplish any work which is presented to them. Every person should have in their soul the absolute disposition to serve God, in the same way as the Angels and more advanced Brothers are ready to help everyone, regardless of their condition.

You ask: In which direction should we turn when we pray? You should know that prayer is not subject to any rule or limitation. When people pray correctly, they are always turned towards God.

You cannot pray if you are not turned towards God. If you are praying to God and at the same time are thinking of someone else – your friend, your mother or your father – you are in fact praying to them instead. If you pray to God and think of your money or your house – you are praying to them. If you pray to God and think of some saint, you are praying to that saint and not to God. Consequently, if you want your prayer to be received by God, your thought should be turned exclusively towards Him. During prayer, your mind should be free of any other thought. Thus, when you pray, it is the Image of God which must be in your mind; no other image. You think: We do not know the Image of God. Yes, you do know that image: but you have forgotten it and must now recall it.

There are moments in life when all beings – from the smallest to the greatest – direct their thought towards God. For human beings, the mystical side of prayer is the choice of that moment, so as to unite it with this general prayer and say: 'I direct my thought, my heart, my soul and my spirit towards the One to Whom everything is now being directed'. Each person will direct a thought which corresponds to their development. God will respond to this collective prayer by sending to each one the necessary light.

Now let us all say the Good Prayer and direct our thought towards the One to Whom everyone is directed this evening. This prayer is general – not only for humanity, but also for the whole universe: for the Angels,

Archangels, Powers, and Dominions. Only in this way will we receive the Divine Blessing in order to grow and develop according to His Will.

THE LORD'S PRAYER
Text, and Commentary
by the Master

Our Father, who art in heaven, hallowed be Thy Name, Thy Kingdom come, Thy Will be done on earth as it is in heaven.

Give us this day our daily bread, and forgive us our trespasses, as we forgive those who trespass against us.

Lead us not into temptation*, but deliver us from evil, for Thine is the Kingdom, the Power and the Glory, for ever and ever.

Amen

In your free and peaceful moments try to concentrate and say the prayer Our Father very slowly. Stop after each phrase you have said, and consider its meaning. During these intervals, new ideas will come, bringing you knowledge which will be useful to you. Little benefit is gained from the rapid and mechanical way in which you recite Our Father and all your prayers.

Another good rule is not to go straight into physical or intellectual activities after you have established the link with the Divine world, with the Love of the Creator, by means of your thought, your heart and your soul. Remain centred for a moment within yourself, in a calm and receptive state, confidently awaiting a blessing or a resonance to the request you have formulated during your prayer.

---

* The Master explained informally to some disciples that this phrase should read 'When in temptation, deliver us from evil'. See commentary below.

In the same way, when someone asks you a question, do not hurry into an immediate response. Reflect, concentrate, listen to your higher self, to what God says to you in this connection, and then make your reply.

Our Father is the first and best prayer. Next comes *The Good Prayer*, which contains ten keys to ten acquisitions.

Our Father – .These two words make us think: God being our Father, the Creator of everything, means that we all form part of a Great Universal Brotherhood. The 'Our' brings to mind the idea of working for the establishment of brotherhood on earth; this must be the supreme ideal of our spirit, of all our spiritual activity, the ideal of all those beings ready to partake of the new culture which is establishing itself on this planet. By calling God 'Father', it follows that every being is an offspring of the divine.

Who art in heaven – By heaven is meant the Divine world. Behind physical life there is a spiritual life, whose roots are plunged in the Divine world. The forces which guide the manifestations of the human world come from the Divine level, by means of the higher spiritual level. God – the Universal Spirit – is the source of the whole of Creation. Behind visible forms we should discover the presence of Divine Thought.

By the words: *Hallowed be Thy Name* we express the will to glorify God by manifesting His Love, that is to say His Name. Love is the only force which links us to the Universal Creator; it is this link of love which gives us strength and health, which sustains us through the long path of our existence.

If we look at our neighbour with the eyes of Love, we discover the beauty in which the human soul lives, which is as yet not visible to everyone. The ideal of our soul is to discover and love God in our neighbour; this is a science which you should think about and apply. Through it a new light will shine in your mind, revealing to you the keys of the hidden powers of Living Nature and raising you to the heights of the knowledge of life.

It is by means of the great idea of the Love of God through our neighbour that the true and longed for unification of humanity will come about. In order to harmonise yourself with someone, try to think of the Divine deposited within them, and love this Divine element; you will then see that this person will begin to love you. As disciples of the new life try to practise this art of loving impartially, without asking yourself whether the person deserves it or not; thus you will be trying out the law, the force of genuine Love. As long as you measure out your love and direct it in an exclusive way, you will always have a limited idea of things.

Every impulse in the new culture will come from Love and gratitude towards life. From now on, when you are asked something, reflect for a moment in order to hear the inner voice of Love; be receptive to its sacred inspiration and act according to its command; you will then feel satisfied that you have accomplished the will of God.

The Love of God is infinite and unlimited; it is the eternal source of Life. By the words 'Hallowed by Thy Name' we mean that Love will be the basis of the new life; it is the key with which the new person will open every door.

Thy Kingdom come – The Kingdom of God is the application of Love to the light of Wisdom. After the words 'Hallowed be Thy Name' comes the phrase 'Thy Kingdom come', which means that we ask for Wisdom to show us the best methods of applying Love, by means of which we hallow the Name of God.

The lessons and lectures of the School of the New Teaching give us the principles of a more advanced culture, of a more beautiful, healthy and harmonious life – the culture of the Sons and Daughters of God. It is said in the scriptures: 'Seek ye first the Kingdom of God and His Justice, and all else will be added unto you'. The fact that God lives in all beings means that justice demands that we respect and esteem everything, with pure and brotherly feelings. Maybe someone is not yet developed, but God knows what they can become! Justice also demands a fair distribution of goods between all; simply by coming to earth, each person has certain rights to appropriate conditions for development.

The words 'Thy Kingdom come' also means that, in the new social order, no living being will be deprived of the conditions of life favourable to their development, growth and well-being; the future society will give people these optimum conditions. If anyone deprives another of their rights as a citizen of human life, they are violating divine justice and are responsible for the delay the coming of the Good.

Thy Will be done – This phrase concerns the Truth. One can see that through the prayer *Our Father* we are asking for help in the realisation of the three fundamental principles of the Great Universal Brotherhood: Love, Wisdom and Truth.

This phrase 'Thy Will be done' means two things:

1. The desire to give God the possibility of manifesting through us more and more, giving Him a greater and greater place in our aspirations and achievements. The higher we climb in the scale of evolution, the more the Divine can manifest in us through expressions of a higher degree.

   If we observe the different kingdoms of Nature – mineral, vegetable, animal, human and angelic – we see that the Spirit of God manifests most incompletely; and to the highest degree in the angelic hierarchy. Angels know nothing more sublime than serving God. Fulfilling the will of God also means consciously working on the development of the capacities and gifts which He has deposited in us. Such is the meaning of the parable of the talents in the Gospel of Luke, chapter 19, vv. 12–27.

2. 'Thy Will be done' also means constantly feeling oneself a servant of God in all our manifestations, desires and impulses. By doing everything for the Lord, with love and discernment, we will notice a great change in our mind and heart, and also in our surroundings. We will be linked with the eternal Universal Divine Source, which can transform and improve everything!

On earth as it is in heaven – In Heaven there is an ideal order and perfect conditions of life; this order should also come down and be established on earth. In order for this to come about, we must strive, with all our strength, to apply

and manifest more and more completely the three principles of Love, Wisdom and Truth.

By means of the phrase *Give us this day our daily bread* we
should consciously recognise that everything we have at our
disposal is a gift from God. The 'daily bread' is also the
Word of God – this is the spiritual meaning of the phrase.

One of the ways in which God speaks inwardly to us is
through our impulses and spiritual aspirations. These
impulses of the Spirit are a powerful lever, encouraging us
to raise ourselves in the sublime path of perfection; we
should pay particular attention to them, since they consti-
tute the 'Word of God'; this is 'Our Daily Bread which
comes down from Heaven' for which we ask in the prayer.
The soul of every being can grasp this Word and feed on
this Bread. All noble desires, every beautiful aspiration or
inclination come from this Voice. In order to hear it, you
need to create a profound inner stillness because God
always speaks to us very softly.

On hearing this gentle fatherly voice, the soul opens and
expands. You feel close to all beings – they are dear to you;
you feel at one with the whole Creation, and ready to do
anything for God. The disciple of the new life grasps a new
idea every day , a clearer ray of the Divine Sun. In the
morning, when you wake up, listen to the first thought
which comes to you from Above; it prepares your heart and
will for work. Listen carefully and gratefully to this early
morning message. Through the words 'Give us this day our
daily bread' we are asking to be instructed by the 'Word',
to discern Divine Wisdom in all created things, in everything which surrounds us, because these are the pages of

the Great Divine Book.

Forgive us our trespasses as we forgive those who trespass against us – In spite of our weaknesses and faults, God's love for us never changes. If, after you have forgiven someone, you do not continue to love those who have offended you, your forgiveness is incomplete and insincere. The offender, the person who does bad things, does so from lack of understanding; he may be intelligent and educated, but he has not yet understood the great meaning of life. The sublime example of true forgiveness was given us by Christ on the cross when he said: 'Father forgive them, for they know not what they do' (Luke 23, v. 34). God sends His Love to everyone; but when people do not forgive one another, they set up an obstacle between God and themselves, an obstacle which prevents Divine Love from reaching them. God has not stopped sending out His Blessing – the Love of God is changeless – but the real cause is in the person who has severed the link.

And lead us not into temptation – As mentioned above, the alternative rendering of this phrase is 'When in temptation', implying that the Lord does not actually lead us into temptation; 'we ask the Lord by these words to give us wisdom and to help us not succumb to temptation through ignorance or stupidity'.

But deliver us from evil – backward spirits can seize hold of a person whose consciousness is not awakened. A person's link with God through prayer and purity of thought and action protects them from bad influences.

For Thine is the Kingdom, the Power and the Glory – Here the Kingdom means Wisdom, the Power Truth and the Glory Love. We affirm here that the Wisdom, Truth and Love of God are unique and true – there is no other. By means of these eternal and active forces, every being will reach perfection and contribute to the realisation of the Sublime Work of God in all its fullness, beauty and power.

PRAYERS

MY BELIEF

I believe in Thee, Lord, who hast spoken to me in the past.

I believe in Thee, Lord, who speaks to me now.

I believe in Thee, Lord, who will speak to me in the future.

May Thy Name be glorified, and may we live in Thy Glory.

May Thy Kingdom be established and may we partake in Thy joy.

May Thy Will be done on earth, as it is in heaven, and may we work together with Thee.

Amen – So Be It!

THE NEW CREDO

I believe in the One Eternal True GOD, who hath spoken to me in the past, who speaks to me in the present, and who will speak to me in the future.

I believe in the Lord and His Spirit, who created the conditions for my salvation.

I believe in the Lord Jesus Christ who came to save the world.

Amen

THE SMALL PRAYER

Lord, my God,
Make me to see Thy Face.
Gladden me for the sake of Thy Name.
Bless me for the sake of Thy Mercy.
Enlighten me for the sake of Thy Spirit.
Exalt me for the sake of Thy Word.
Help me for the sake of Thy Promise.
Guide me for the sake of Thy Truth.
Support me for the sake of Thy Justice.
Blessed art Thou, Lord, for ever,
For Thou art kind and Truthful towards all.

Amen

THE GOOD PRAYER

The Good Prayer is not only for humanity, but for the whole Universe, for all angels, archangels, dominions, thrones and powers

The Master

Lord God, our tender Heavenly Father, who hast given given us life and health to rejoice in Thee, send us Thy Spirit to protect us, to shield us from every harm and from all evil thoughts.

Teach us to do Thy Will, to sanctify Thy Name, to glorify Thee at all times.

Sanctify our spirits, enlighten our hearts and minds to keep Thy decrees and commandments.

Inspire us with Thy holy presence and pure thoughts, direct us in Thy ways, so that we may serve Thee with joy.

Bless the life we consecrate to Thee for the sake of our brothers and sisters, and those dear to us.

Succour us and assist us, so that we may grow in Wisdom and understanding, that we may be instructed by Thy Word and that we may abide in Thy Truth.

Guide us in all our thoughts and actions in Thy Name, so that Thy Kingdom may come on earth.

Feed our souls with Thy Heavenly bread and fill us with Thy strength, so that our lives may be fruitful.

And as Thou dost shower us with all Thy blessings, may Thy Love remain our eternal law.

For Thine is the Kingdom, the Power and the Glory, for ever and ever.

Amen

PRAYER OF THE HOLY SPIRIT

O Lord our God, our souls trust in Thee, hear my supplication and give heed to my prayer. Elevate my spirit and give comfort to my heart. Show me the light of Thy face.

Lord, for the sake of Thy mercy, support me with the presence of Thy Spirit.

Lord, may Thy Kingdom come, my Thy Justice be done, may Thy Truth prevail, may Thy Love be established, and may you, Lord Jesus Christ, the Only-Begotten Son of God, dwell in your fullness within my soul.

And may the Glory of the Lord God our Father be manifest in the Spirit of His Word throughout all ages.

Amen

PRAYER ON THE PATH OF LIFE

O Lord, our God and Saviour, of every strength and refuge, of every Truth and Love, of every state and authority, source of all blessings in our life, send us Thy gentle Spirit to guide and sustain us in the Path of life, to enlighten our minds and to illuminate our hearts, to give us strength and life, so that we may accomplish Thy good Will.

Forgive us our transgressions, which we confess before Thee – they have estranged us from Thy Fatherly Love. Blot them out of the book of Thy remembrances, and grant us the peace of the Spirit.

Make Thy Face now to shine upon us that we may be an image of Thy Love, heralds of Thy Truth and servants of Thy Righteousness.

Bless this nation among whom we live, bless our brothers and sisters with whom we work. Bless all mothers and fathers who do Thy Will, listen to the voice of all those who suffer on the face of the earth and bless them.

Bless our Master who leads us in Thy Sacred Path. Blessed art Thou, O Lord our God, blessed be Thy Name for all Eternity, for Thou art the Way, the Truth and the Life, there is no other God but Thee. Thou art the only ONE.

Amen

PRAYER OF THE TRIUNE GOD

i

Lord, may Thy Spirit come upon my spirit to fill my heart and soul with Thy presence and to strengthen my feet in all justice.

I bow before the Eternal rock, out of which I have been carved.

Blessed is Thy Name, Lord, strengthen me and exalt me, so that I may serve Thee with gladness.

ii

O Lord my God, may Thy Spirit come to enlighten my mind, illuminate my heart and fill my soul with every joy and exaltation.

I bow before Thee, the Eternal Source, who hast always redeemed me. Wash my feet, cleanse my heart and deliver my soul, so that I may be pure and sacred before Thee.

Blessed art Thou, O Lord my God.

iii

O Lord my God, may Thy blessing come upon my spirit. May my heart and my soul be filled with the blessed fruits of the Spirit, may my feet be made firm with the strength of Thy presence.

I bow before Thy Eternal Spirit which vivifies me and resurrects me from the dead.

Protect me, Lord, and strengthen me with Thy Holy Name, so that I may serve Thee with joy and gladness and that I may become one with Thee, Lord Jesus Christ, as Thou art one with the Father.

Amen

PRAYER OF THE KINGDOM

Lord, our God, may my supplication arise before Thy face, may Thy Kingdom come and may Thy Word abide in our hearts according to Thy Love, with which Thou hast cherished us.

Tender Heavenly Father, Abba, may Thy Kingdom come, may Thy Will be done, may Thy Name shine on Earth. Such is the desire of our soul, the need which we constantly feel in this world.

Great Lord of every strength and refuge, stand firm in Thy Cause, bend the hearts of all those whom Thou hast chosen so as to call forth the germ of Thy Glory and Greatness.

Kindly Lord, lead us with Thy merciful hands, enlighten us so that we do not err and stray from Thy Word, so that we do not transgress Thy law.

Lead us like a good shepherd in green pastures and by clear streams.

Thou One Supreme Lord and Saviour of the World, known before all the centuries of Light.

One with the shining Light* of our life, vouchsafe our soul to expand, our spirit to grow, our heart to be reborn, our mind to be enlightened, so that we may glorify Thee now and for ever.

Amen.

* *In Bulgarian there are two words for light:* videlina *for spiritual light and* cvetlina *for physical light. Here* videlina *is used.*

PRAYER OF THE FRUITS
OF THE SPIRIT

God of Tenderness, God of Love, we call upon Thy Mercy. We accept the sufferings which Thou sendest us with joy in our heart. We accept the hardships which Thou sendest for the strengthening of our spirit. We will fulfil Thy good Will without hesitating or vacillating.

Send us Thy Spirit, to bring into our hearts, our minds and our souls the fruit of Love, the good of joy and peace, the foundation of Thy patience and gentleness.

Give us the gift of Faith, mildness and restraint. Bless us as Thou hast always blessed us. Make Thy Name dear to our souls. Establish Thy Kingdom in our souls. Feed our souls with Thy Word, to sustain in us all Thy virtues. May Thy Radiant Spirits of Love, Faith and Hope be present within us, now and for ever, together with Thee.

We bring Thee praise, Glory be to Thee, the One Lord and God of the Great Sacrifice.

Amen.

PRAYER TO THE SUPREME BEING

O boundless Supreme Being, I beseech Thee to allow me to come near to Thee and to be very close to Thee, infinitely close, so that I may feel myself to be an essential part of the wholeness of Existence, and may I become aware of myself as a complete being that has sprung from Thee.

Liberate me from all wrongful thoughts, feelings, desires, doubts, criticisms and reproaches. And may I be as humble as Thou hast created me.

May I feel Thee very close to myself as a close friend from whom I may never part. Be Thou a light in my mind so that I may see Thee in it, be Thou life in my heart so that I see Thee within it, as I see Thee outside myself.

May I know only Thy eternal laws in nature and in the whole universe, and may Thy ceaseless Love unite me with Thee throughout all ages.

Amen

THE PRAYER OF SACRED PURITY

Lord, our God of all our inner fullness of life, we stand before Thy face, according to Thy great mercy, which brings the light of Thy face, a gift for our souls.

We have purified our mouths and Thy Glory fills our speech. We glorify Thee, we praise Thee. Thy tender Spirit cleanses our hearts and we exalt Thy name and receive the great joy which it brings into our lives.

May Thy Great Spirit cleanse our minds and may the boundless desire to work for the glory of Thy Holy Name be born within us, so that we may spread Thy Great conceptions throughout the whole world. Thou hast cleansed our souls and the sacred yearning for eternity in which Thou dwellest is born within us, so that we may work for the good of our dear ones, and for the good of our souls.

According to Thy mercy, which is uniquely Thine, bless us, illuminate us, lift us up, strengthen us, resurrect us and fill our souls with Thy kind Spirit, so that we may always serve Thee with joy and gladness. May we carry the image of Thy Love, the light of Thy Truth, the harmony of Thy Wisdom, the foundation of Thy Goodness and the Purity of Thy Justice.

Amen

Given on September 23rd, 1923

PRAYER OF THE SPIRIT OF GOD

Lord, our God, may Thy Kind Spirit come and enfold and embrace our spirit in Thy arms to fill our hearts with the boundless Love which proclaims Thy presence throughout the world, to strengthen our hands in all justice and our feet in all goodness.

We bow down before Thee, our Eternal Father, the Rock of our lives.

Blessed art Thou, blessed is Thy Name in our souls.

Strengthen us, lift us up, so that we may begin to serve the coming of Thy Kingdom with all gladness for the Love which Thou hast shown towards us!

Thou art the only one Who knows us, and we know that Thou art the light of our souls, the reach of our minds, the extent of our strength, the fortress of our spirits and the fullness of our hearts.

Thou art the adornment and glory in our lives!

Amen

PRAYER GIVEN BY THE MASTER ON THE FIRST EVENING IN VARNA
19th August 1903

I thank Thee, my God, for the great Love with which Thou hast loved us, we thank Thee for the life Thou hast given us, we thank Thee for the mind Thou hast instilled in us.

We thank Thee for the virtue which Thou hast placed as a foundation within us.

We thank Thee for the virtue which Thou hast placed as a foundation in our life.

We thank Thee for the justice with which Thou hast surrounded us, we thank Thee for the Love with which Thou hast filled us.

We thank Thee for the Great Wisdom and glorify Thee for Thy Truth, with which Thou hast illuminated us.

We rejoice in the life which Thou hast given us and we fulfil Thy Will.

Now, in accordance with the Spirit which Thou hast given us to guide us, bless us all now and always.

Amen

Note: *The prayer on the preceding page dates from the first congress in Varna, attended by three disciples. The Master explained that many beings from the invisible world were also in attendance, and turned to the three to say: 'Now you are three, but in the future you will be many'.*

PRAYER FOR OUR TIMES

Lord, my God, Great and Holy Teacher of all Love and Wisdom, of every mercy and justice, hear the prayer of those who turn to Thee at these fateful times.

Tender Lord, with Thy Great Love forgive the transgressions of mankind, enlighten our minds, cleanse our hearts, strengthen our faith, awaken our souls, so that we may all come to know Thee and fulfil Thy Fatherly Will.

Lead us out of the dark valley of our ignorance, pride and sin. Give us peace, and illuminate us with Thy Truth. Give us the gift of Thy Love and show us the true path of our lives. May Thy Peace which has vanished return to the world. Give light to all, so that we may cast aside every lie, every vice, every conflict and violence, so that human thoughts of war may be banished for ever. May the nations of the world come to know that Thou art our One Heavenly Father, that mankind is one family, and that Thy Love and Thy Law are the true path of our lives.

Father, send us saints, prophets and geniuses, as Thou hast sometimes done in the past, so that they may lead the nations throughout the world. Transmit through Thy kind thought that the world may be inherited by the meek and may the Love of good people become the rock of human brotherhood.

Our Great Master, Spirit of the ever kindly God, prepare us for the abundant harvest of the Holy Divine Initiative, for which Thou hast worked in the world. According to Thy Divine plan, strengthen us through all the heavenly angels and saints who are the true servants of the Universal Brotherhood of Light.

Enlighten us to work with all good people. Give knowledge, faith and strength to the sowers of Thy seed in the world and to all whom Thou hast called so that we may fulfil Thy task to its end. May the nation amongst whom we work, the chosen Slavic people, fulfil Thy Divine Will. May the Slavs be a beacon and fortress of the Divine Initiative among the nations and may the Divine plan be fully manifest in the world.

May the Will of God be done. May the Kingdom of God come, and may Thou, our Father, live for ever in the souls of all mankind.

Amen

PRAYER OF THE DISCIPLE
THE GOOD PATH

Lord of light, of every abundance and gentleness, about whom my Master has spoken to me and who speaks about Thee, reveal Thyself to me as Thou deignest, as it is pleasing to Thee.

I am ready to do Thy Will without any deviation, without any hesitation, without any doubt.

Thus I will be loyal and truthful, as Thou art loyal and truthful.

For the sake of the name of my Master, through whom Thou hast spoken to me, may I always rejoice in the presence of Thy Word, in the manifestation of Thy Great and Sacred Spirit so as to be always like the little children of Thy Kingdom – obedient, conscientious, constant, patient and always content in Thy boundless Love, which Thou hast shown towards all the weak and infirm who seek the path of Thy Eternal Light in which Thou dwellest.

Enlighten me, I pray Thee, O Lord. Let not the presence of Thy Gentle Spirit move away from my Soul, from my mind, from my will, so as to do always what is pleasing to Thee.

May Thy Spirit dwell in my soul, may I rejoice in the presence of Thy Light for the sake of the Name of my Master with whose name Thou art known in the world.

Amen

PRAYERS FOR PEACE

God of Love, may Thy Will be done on earth. May there be peace between all the nations.

Lord, illuminate with Thy Light all minds, hearts and souls, so that they may be penetrated with the idea of brotherhood, mutual cooperation and Love between the nations of the earth.

Amen

Lord, our God, may Thy Kingdom come on earth as it is in heaven, and may all nations whom you have called take their place in Thy Kingdom, so that they may serve Thee with joy and gladness.

Amen

LOSINKA

Note: Losinka *is a diminutive form of* losa, *which means 'vine'.*

O Lord, bless and strengthen my soul!

i

We pray to our Heavenly Father for the glorified and sanctified Name of the Lord, our God on earth among mankind and among the believers and among those chosen from the order of the Glory of the Lord, the Saviour, the Protector who raises and resurrects the dead and establishes law and order everywhere. And blessed be the Name of the Lord Jesus Christ – the Manifested Word of God and with Him all those who Love Him.

ii

We pray to our Heavenly Father for the coming of the Kingdom of God on earth among the people and in the hearts of believers and in the souls of the chosen ones so that every justice, every good, every Love, every Wisdom, every Truth be put into action; and may the Lord our God come to reign and may the words of the Lord be carried out: 'The Lord has deigned to give you a Kingdom'.

And may the Spirit of the Lord Jesus Christ be instilled among us and may the preordained intention of our Father of Light and of the Radiant Spirits be fulfilled and may there be glory and honour and adoration towards Him throughout all ages.

iii

We pray to our Heavenly Father for the fulfilment of the Will of our Lord God on earth, as it is in heaven, among the Bright Angelic Faces, and may the law of Truth, Love and Justice be established so that we may all be one body and one spirit and may there be order, harmony and praise so that He may give us knowledge to glorify Him and rejoice in Him and his Deeds. And may He be instilled in our lives and in the work of our hands, and may all those who trust in him have life, health and longevity. And deliver us from all the deeds of the evil and sly one. And bring peace into my soul. And give them the abundance of Thy blessings.

And may the Lord remember His promises, may He have mercy on all those who suffer, may He bless all believers, may He strengthen His chosen ones, may He give strength, knowledge, Wisdom and Love to prevail in His Name and His Holy Name.

May He ultimately give us Victory over our enemies, so that we may serve the Lord with joy and gladness throughout all the days of our life. May we be illumined by His Face to strengthen and fortify us. May we accomplish His Good Will.

May we come before Him with fullness, in wisdom and equanimity. May He make all our suffering brothers and sisters whole, bless them, their homes and their children.

May He bless all the good initiatives of their souls and spirits.

And thus may our God be exalted within us as He is in heaven.

Amen.

PRAYERS FOR THE DECEASED

i

L ord, grant Thy peace to the soul of _____, which it hath pleased Thee to take away. May he/she be placed in Thy most radiant celestial spheres. Endow him/her with Thy spiritual virtues so that he/she may be raised to see Thy Glory and Grandeur. May his/her soul rejoice in Thy Kindness and Love.

Grant them eternal peace, Lord and may eternal light shine on their souls. (*3 times*)

Amen.

ii

G ive Thy peace, Lord, and remember Thy deceased servant _____, forgive all his/her wrongdoing when on this earth, voluntary and involuntary, in thought, word and deed, forgive him/her, and may he/she dwell in radiant, pure and peaceful spheres, where there is no illness, no sorrow, no sighing, where there is boundless eternal life.

Lord, forgive him/her, Lord, remember him/her in Thy Heavenly Kingdom. Lord, raise him/her into the light. May God give him/her peace and light. Peace for his/her ashes, tranquillity for his/her spirit, and light for his/her soul.

Amen

iii

Lord of Universal mercy, Thou who hast created man to live on the earth and who hast instilled Thy Spirit within him so that Thou mayest raise him up to Thyself, we entreat Thee now to hear our prayer, remember our (brother or sister) who has passed into the other world, remember all our deceased brothers, sisters, fathers, mothers, sons and daughters, close and distant relatives and all good people, and bless them with Thy great Blessing.

Give joy to those souls and inspire in them the hope that thou wilt soon send them back to the earth to continue their evolution to full realisation, so that they may complete the work of Thy Salvation.

Lord, we rejoice that Thou hast made it possible for us to intercede with Thee for our deceased dear ones and in the confidence that our prayer will be heard by Thee and that they will delight in the joy which they have long been awaiting.

Blessed be Thou, O Lord, blessed be Thy Name now and throughout the ages.

Amen

iv

Lord, give light and peace to our beloved brother (or sister) _____ Straighten his/her path, as Thou leadest him/her towards Thee. Illuminate his/her path with light, send him/her souls who will guide him/her, teach and help him/her on the path which leads to Thee.

Lord, receive _____ in Thy Bosom. Surround him/her with Thy boundless Love and lead him/her in the light of Thy Wisdom.

Lord, bless _____ and may he/she grow from love to love, from light to light, from abundance to abundance and from freedom to freedom.

Lord, bless _____

May there be peace on his/her soul and eternal light on his/her path.

Amen

FORMULAS FOR THE DEPARTED

And this is eternal life to know Thee, the One True God, and Christ whom Thou hast sent. (*3 times*)

May there be peace on his/her spirit and eternal light on his/her soul. (*3 times*)

When we pray for the deceased, we read the prayers in the following order:

1. Prayers for the deceased.

2. Silent prayer.

3. Our Father.

4. Psalms 23 and 121.

5. Prayer of Daniel.

6. Chapter 14 of the Gospel of John.

7. Formulas for the departed.

PRAYER OF DANIEL

Blessed be the name of God for ever and ever: for wisdom and might are His: and He changeth the times and the seasons: He removeth kings, and setteth up kings: He giveth wisdom unto the wise, and knowledge to them that know understanding: He revealeth the deep and secret things: He knoweth what is in the darkness, and the light dwelleth with Him.

I thank thee and praise thee, O thou God of my fathers, Who hast given me wisdom and might, and hast made known unto me now what we desired of Thee.

Amen

(Daniel 2, 20–23)

PRAYER FOR EVERY DAY

Lord, illuminate my mind, bless my heart, strengthen my will, my memory, my faith so as to justify my existence and to solve the tasks for which I have come to earth.

Lord, please send Thy Spirit to bring into my heart, my mind and my soul the fruit of Love, the blessings of joy and peace, the foundation of Thy patience and loving kindness.

Amen

MORNING PRAYER OF THE DISCIPLE
(given in Plovdiv)

Lord God, my soul quivers with joy before the light of the new day which illuminates my path.

I thank Thee for having woken me at this early hour when Thou art glorified by the wise, the birds and the pure flowers.

I thank Thee for making me a gift of another day of life, and for calling me to pursue my work on earth, healthy and restored.

I thank Thee for giving me the chance to accomplish Thy good Will, to manifest it with love and wisdom by serving my brothers and sisters.

I beseech Thee to give me the sense of presence of Thy Divine Spirit, to listen to Thy guidance like a devoted child and that my soul may not stray from the path of Thy laws.

Grant me the strength, the vigilance and the love to live for my elevation and that of all humanity and all creatures and for the coming of the Divine Kingdom on Earth.

May the light of the Eternal Sun of Thy Love illuminate my soul and those of all my brothers and sisters on the face of the earth!

May the light of the Eternal Sun of Thy Love illuminate the whole of humanity and all creatures for the
coming of the Divine Kingdom on earth.

May Thy Love, Thy Wisdom, Thy Truth, Thy
Justice and Thy Virtues begin to reign in the life of
mankind!

May all human beings become One with Christ and
the radiant angels, One with Thee and the Universal
Brotherhood of Light!

Amen

MORNING PRAYERS

I thank Thee, Lord, for protecting me so kindly during this night. Help me not to aggrieve Thee with any sin so that I may spend this day safely and pleasing Thee

Amen.

I thank Thee, Lord, for giving me life and health. Fill my heart with love,and strengthen my will, so that I may accomplish Thy Will. May everything I do be done in Thy Name and for Thy Glory.

Amen

Lord, I ask Thee to fill me with the energies of life. May they penetrate every cell of my body by bringing it strength and health; may they strengthen my spirit in accomplishing the task assigned to me on earth.

Amen

Lord, I thank Thee for the gift of life so that I may serve Thee today. Bless my soul, O Lord. I thank Thee that I have risen today to accomplish my work as I should. Wherever I go, may I grow as much as I should.

Amen

May Love, Faith and Hope unite in our hearts and may the Lord be glorified in our souls.

Amen

I will serve the Lord with my mind, my heart and my strength. I will walk in the Lord's path with my Love, my faith and my strength and I will come to know God in my life with my heart and my mind.

Amen

Lord, Thou hast sent me to the earth, Thou hast given me life and health, thou hast given me my mind, heart and life. I will fulfil Thy Will, I will glorify Thee. And after I fulfil the Will of God, and after God has blessed me, then I will do what is good for my soul and will help those close to me.

Amen

Bless, O Lord, my soul. Cleanse me, God, from evil thoughts. I thank Thee for the great goodness which Thou hast shewn towards me. I know Thee as good, all merciful, all truthful and all wise.

Amen

I thank Thee, Lord, I thank Thee for everything Thou hast given me and taught me.

Amen

PRAYER ON AWAKENING

Lord, lead me towards Thy great understanding, fortified by Thy Good Will!

Lord, bless my brothers and sisters as Thou blessest me. I will serve Thee as Thou teachest me, I will Thy Love according to Thy Will.

I thank Thee, Lord, for everything good which Thou hast given and taught me.

I thank Thee, Master, that Thou hast preserved my life and health today as always!

Amen

PRAYERS BEFORE SLEEP

i

Kindly Lord, this evening I wish to go to study in the school of the Universal Brotherhood of Light. The Lord loves me and I love Him. God is boundless, so He loves me. And in his Love there is absolutely no doubt whatsoever. I will be in heaven, for God has spoken and His word is unchanging.

Lord receive my soul this night in the heavenly school to study, to work and to pray.

Surround my body with a bright circle of light so that it may be protected from every evil and harmful thought.

Without fear in boundless Love!

Amen

ii

Lord our God, Kindly lover of humanity, forgive me any sins of this day in word, deed and thought. Bestow upon me a peaceful and tranquil sleep. Send Thy Angel guardian to protect and shield me from all evil, for Thou art the guardian of our souls and bodies and to Thee – Father, Son and Holy Spirit, we give Glory now and always, for ever and ever.

Amen

NIGHT PRAYER

Teach me, Lord, about Thy law, illuminate my soul, enlighten my mind, ennoble my heart so that I may manifest as Thou desirest, so that I may attune my life to Thy laws, to Thy principles, so as to inherit Thy life.

Lord, I am illuminated by the rays of Thy Love, I call out to Thee with a joyful voice: Great art Thou, our Kindly Heavenly Father!

Pour upon us the blessings of Thine Eternal Spirit, so that we may see Thee and serve Thee always!

Lord, in the early morning dawn, when we reflect on Thee and Thy Greatness, beams of light pour forth like a crystal clear stream into my mind and form a sacred thread which links me to Thee, my Father!

Therefore I feel Thee close to me and I receive Thy help, which sustains me. And like a clear Source of pure influences which are now appearing countless before me, wafting the sweetness of the whole Universe before me, my soul is awakened and swims in bliss and begins to sing in adoration: Praise be to Thy Great Name, King of Eternity!...

And thus, Lord, the morning reflections teach me Thy laws.

When everything is still in an enchanted sleep, the rays of the as yet unrisen sun pour into and gently stroke every soul so as to initiate a new, pure and sacred life.

Lord, Thou art our supreme hope!

Therefore, when we are permeated by purity, when the spirit of Thy eternity illuminates our path with light, we are content, joyful and give thanks. So join us with Thy Spirit, O Lord!

Amen

(Prayer given during August 1937 in the village of Kableshkovo.)

SHORT PRAYERS

Lord, we thank Thee for this beautiful life, for this beautiful world which Thou hast created for us, we wish to live according to that Love, which Thou has placed in our souls.

Amen

May Thy Light enlighten our minds. With this light we will resolve that Divine question which now sits before the door of our souls.

Amen

Lord, we thank Thee for this beautiful life, for this beautiful world, which Thou hast created around us, we wish to live according to this love which Thou hast placed in our souls.

Amen

May Thy Light enlighten our minds. With this light may we solve that Divine question which sits before the door of our souls.

Amen

Most kindly Lord, pour the light of Divine Wisdom into my mind, so that I may understand Thy laws; immerse my heart in the warmth of Thy Love, so that I may accomplish the smallest good deed and illuminate my path towards Thee

70

with the radiance of Divine Truth, so that I may
return to Thy Bosom and fulfil Thy Will.

Amen

Lord, may no lie come forth from my lips, I will
speak only Truth. I will fulfil only that which
Thou wishest. I will not spend my life doing nothing.

I will willingly accomplish all Thy wishes. I will fol-
low Thee not because Thou hast made Heaven and
Earth, but because Thou art Unique, Infinite and
Eternal, Who contains everything within Thyself.

Bless me, O Lord. I thank Thee for all Thou hast
given me and for all Thou hast taught me. Help me
to increase the freedom of my soul, the strength of
my spirit, the light of my mind and the goodness of
my heart.

Amen

I thank Thee, Lord, for the great blessing which
Thou givest us. We know Thee as Ever-merciful,
Ever-wise, Ever-loving and Ever-kind.

Amen

PRAYER OF THE DISCIPLES OF THE BROTHERHOOD OF LIGHT

We thank Thee, Lord, that we have been born in this time. We thank Thee, that Thou hast awakened us and called us into the fold of the Brotherhood of Light.

We beseech Thee, through the Power of Thy Spirit, the Great Spirits of the Living God and our contact through Thy Word, that those souls in the world who do not yet know Thee should awaken.

Bless all those who join in Thy Work. Increase their number, so that they may work in the Divine field for the coming of the Kingdom of God on earth.

Amen

PRAYER OF THE DISCIPLE

I have chosen the path of Truth!
I will walk in Thy Truth!
Teach me, Lord, and lead me along Thy Path!
Send me Thy Light and Thy Truth
so that they may guide me!
Give me faith!
I believe in Thee, O Lord.

PRAYER – THE SOURCE OF THE GOOD

Lord, I am ready from now on to fulfil Thy Will, which moves every living creature in the world. If I have found a blessing in Thy presence, may I feel Thy Joy in the name of Thy Love, Wisdom and Truth. Lord, place me in the fire of Thy Love!

Lord, what should I do for the joyful establishment of Thy Kingdom on earth and for the illumination of Thy Name for humanity.

Lord, teach me how to think about my brothers and sisters as Thou thinkest about them.

Amen

THE BEAUTIFUL PRAYER
(prayer given to a group of ten people)

Lord God, make us as indestructible as diamonds, so that we may become the foundation of the new universe. Make us like conductors in Thy Living Church, so that we may transmit Divine Life to the people. Illuminate us with the strength of Thy Holy Spirit, so that we may awaken the sleeping souls with Thy words, thoughts and deeds. Reveal in us, dear Lord, Thy Divine essence, help us gather strength, so that we may know the Truth, that we may become children of the light, that we may walk in the path of Justice, for the realisation of Thy Plan for the coming of Thy Kingdom on earth.

Amen

THE PRAYER OF GRATITUDE

We thank Thee, our Father, for the great Love, with which Thou hast loved us. We thank Thee for the Life which Thou hast given us. We thank Thee for the mind which Thou hast placed within us. We thank Thee for the virtues which Thou hast placed as a foundation of our life. We thank Thee for the Justice, with which Thou hast surrounded us. We thank Thee for the Love, with which Thou hast filled us. We thank Thee for Thy Great Wisdom and we glorify Thee for Thy Truth with which Thou hast enlightened us. We rejoice in the life which Thou hast given us and we fulfil Thy Will. Because of the Spirit which Thou hast sent to lead us, blessed art Thou by all of us now and for evermore.

Amen

PRAYER FOR SPIRITUAL AND PHYSICAL HEALTH

O God, our Strength and Support, Physician of all physicians, bearer of all heavenly wellbeing and freshness, come and live within me and cleanse me from all impurities. Wash away all harmful influence from evil and mischievous spirits, save my body and soul. Make my body Thy temple, and my soul a precious treasure of Thy testaments and virtues.

When Thou cleansest out every evil stain from my soul and erasest my former sins and actions, spread over me Thy miraculous blessing and life-giving strength, when Thou givest me health and persistence to overcome hindrances and fatigue.

Remove far from me every harmful desire, every gloomy thought expressed by our antagonist, for Thou art God, the Physician beyond physicians – the wisest and the mightiest.

Amen

PRAYER OF THE HOLY SPIRIT
FOR THE ILL

If one is within Christ, one is created anew.
And all these blessings will come to you
and remain with you.
And I will heal you.
We are one body and One Spirit!
I am the Lord who will heal you.
Be purified!
Lord, be merciful towards me, a sinner!
Heal my soul and caress me!
Pray for each other so that you may be healed.
The supplication which is made with faith will heal
the suffering ..... (*name*)

Amen

*The following psalms are said for healing: 102, 40, 35,
91, 70, 86, 88, 97, 115, 116. And for the mentally ill,
Psalm 57.*

PRAYERS FOR HEALING

i

Lord, Thou art the source of life! Send me the life-giving Power of Thy Spirit in order to heal my mind, my heart, my spirit, my soul, my will and my body. May I be healed of every physical and psychological illness and suffering. Endow me with health, strength and life, with youth and beauty; may there grow within me gifts and capacities so that I may live, learn and serve Thee!

Amen

ii

Ever-present and ever-kindly God, in the Name of the Lord who hath spoken with Thy servant, may Thy healing come through us, Thy servants, for the glory of Thy Name.

We thank Thee that Thou hast listened to us. Thou only art our Lord, and there is none other than Thee.

Thou art the One who can always heal, and Thy healing is health for the soul and the body. Restore the harmonious operation between mind and soul, between soul and body.

Turn the source of the heart to useful work – for the good and strength of the body .

May this our brother (sister), who is suffering, receive Thy mercy, so that we may all rejoice in the presence of Thy strength.

Amen

This prayer should be said every Wednesday, Saturday and Sunday morning at seven and nine o'clock.

PRAYER FOR THE ILL

Lord of the strong, Thou art our refuge from birth to birth. We glorify Thy mercies throughout the ages. Thou hast made a covenant with Thy chosen ones, because Thou hast a supportive and strong hand to grant mercy to those who know Thee in Thy Name.

Turn, O Lord Thy countenance towards those who suffer (our brother or sister), give heed to the sufferings and relieve them. We have great faith in Thy words, for Thou hast said: 'Turn towards Me and I will answer you, for I am your Lord who supports your right hand, and I say to you: "Do not be anxious, I will help you. Do not be anxious, for I chose you and called you by your name. You are not alone when you pass through the water, I shall be with you when you go through the fire, you will not be burned and the flames will not scorch you, and do not be anxious in infirmity, for I am with you!"'

And now hear our entreaty, Lord, pour out of the abundance of Thy mercy!

Amen

PRAYER FOR FASTING

May God transform and wreck those enemies and all evil thoughts which hinder and impede the Divine Plan.

May His Name be glorified on Earth as it is in Heaven.

Amen

PRAYER OF THE CHILD

Protect me, O God, our Daddy, to bear all misfortunes and to recover my innocence from constant temptations.

Bless my bread and air and pure water and give me childlike sleep – pure and sweet, so as to be strong and steadfast in work.

Sweet Creator, pour Thy Love generously into my young heart, may I help in all suffering and walk in Thy new path.

Thou Who canst do everything and cares unceasingly for little birds and for the peace of the whole world, O God, watch over from Thy heavenly vault, send Thy blessing upon my young life, to grow beneath Thy abundance, beneath Thy bright space, to awaken with joy and fall asleep with peace!

Amen

PRAYER OF THE ELECT

Lord, bless this nation, protect it, raise it, give it courage, protect its spirit, give it faith, confidence, hope in Thee to awaken and to glorify Thee throughout all future ages.

Accomplish, Lord, our God, according to Thy Great Name, by which Thou hast been known throughout all ages.

Make Thy Name to shine throughout all nations, and may they know that Thou art One, in Whom there is no deceit and Who is always strong to help and redeem.

Disperse our enemies, Lord, from in front of Thy face. We will glorify Thee with a pure heart when Thou helpest us to overcome the cunning spirits of hell, who wish to spoil Thy work.

Thou, Lord, alone dost accomplish this with Thy strong hands.

Do this according to our Lord Jesus Christ, through Whose Name Thou hast blessed us to call upon Thee.

Amen

PRAYER
for those who are discontent with life

Lord, we are discontent with life, so we come before Thee in order to learn how to free ourselves from discontent. Forgive us our discontent. We made a wrong choice in our lives, but the second time we will not make any choice. Hence we will be born of water and the Spirit.

Lord, forgive us that we have done no good to anyone, we have done no good to ourselves, we are great unbelievers.

Lord, Thou who hast created the world, save us and we will live only for Thee from now on.

Thou wilt overcome. Thy victory is my victory.

I believe in One God of Love, in One Teacher of Wisdom, in One Spirit of Truth.

The God of Love is not the God of the dead, but the God of the living.

Amen

PRAYER
against the enemies of the Divine Plan in the world

Lord of the strong, disperse all evil thoughts of the enemies and of all their allies, of all other dark forces which wish to obstruct Thy Sacred Plan for the Earth.

Destroy their intrigues. May it be, Lord, according to Thy word: Mine is the revenge.

May Thy Name be glorified, Lord, in Earth, and may all people know that Thou art the One True God, the Saviour of Peace – Christ. Bless all those who know Thee and serve Thee with Spirit and Truth.

May Thy Fatherly hand of security and protection be amongst those who act in Thy Name.

May Thy Will, Lord, be done on Earth and may Thy Kingdom come on Earth now and throughout all ages.

Amen

PRAYER FOR THE PROSPERITY
OF THE DIVINE INITIATIVE

Lord, enlighten the whole of humanity in the Spiritual chain of being with Thy Light and Strength. May the whole of humanity receive the Teaching of Christ and the Word of the Master! May all believe that there is a GOD!

May the ideas about God grow in every soul, so that whoever preaches godlessness may become jealous of Thy Word so that all the faithless may become faithful!

Lord, we pray to Thee with great zeal. May Thy Divine mercy suffuse the whole earth and may Thy Divine love fill every heart.

Lord, enlighten with Thy Light all peoples and their leaders so that they may be in harmony and agree on all questions so as to bring Thy peace to the world, Lord! Lord, may brotherhood come between all the nations on the face of the Earth.

Lord, bring life, light and renewal to all circles of the Brotherhood of Light throughout the world.

Amen

PRAYER
given in 1925

L ord, we are ready to fulfil Thy Sacred Will without the slightest deviation and our whole joy will
be to serve Thee with our whole heart, with our
whole soul and with our whole spirit.

We wish to know Thee as love within us and outside
of us. May Thou always be in all our undertakings,
in all our thoughts, desires and actions. May Thou
be the alpha and omega of our life. The beginning of
all Thy blessing and the end of all our misunderstandings, the beginning of Truth and the end of
Love, the beginning of Wisdom and the end of fool-
ishness, the beginning of strength and the end of
violence. May Thou be a New Beginning, which is
without beginning and without end.

The beginning of the New Light, of the New Life
which Thou bringest now into our souls. We know
Thee as Thou knowest us, we love Thee as Thou
lovest us, we are one with Thee, as Thou art the
Oneness in that Light.

From now on Thy Love will reign in the fullness of
Thy mercy through all the days of our life. We begin
the New Life. Enter into us and we will come to
Thee. Enter into our souls and bring Thy Light into
the New Life.

Illuminate our new hearts, which Thou hast given us and fill our minds with Thy light, which Thou hast brought into our minds.

And thus our motto is: fear outside and love within, darkness outside and light within.

With love and light we are souls of Love and Light.

Amen

UNIVERSAL PRAYER

Father of all! Through every century, respect at every level: from saints, from primitives, from sages – Jehovah, Jove or Lord! Thou, the Great Primary Principle, I understood who limited all my feelings so that I might, however, know that Thou art kind and that, alone, I am weak. In that gloomy vision, Thou hast already given me to see the good in everything, quickly connecting nature with fate. Thou hast maintained the freedom of the human will. What my conscience tells me to do or warns me not to do, instructs me sooner than escaping evil or pursuing heaven.

Whatever blessing Thy generosity gives in freedom, do not allow it to be cast aside.

For God payment means to be obedient – using whatever a person has learned. But do not allow me to find the limits of Thy goodness, gathered from earthly space, or to think that Thou art the Lord only of humanity, when around us exist thousands of worlds. Do not allow this weak and ignorant hand arrogantly to hurl Thy arrows and to find the damned beneath all who are condemned as Thy enemies.

If I am just – may I transmit Thy blessings, calmly standing within justice. If I err, O teach my heart to find this better path! And forgive me my foolish pride and unfair discontent about things which Thy generosity has refused or things which Thy goodness did not allow.

Teach me to feel the sorrow of others, to conceal the sins, the failings which I see: teach me to show others mercy, although I am small, but not wholly insignificant, since I am enlivened by Thy Breath.

O, lead me wherever I go through life to that day or through death.

May bread and peace be my share on that day.

Everything else under the sun Thou knowest better is given or not.

And may Thy Will be done.

Towards Thee, whose temple is space, whose altar is the earth, the sea, the heavens.

May the whole of Being raise one chorus of praise!

May the incense of the whole of Nature rise towards Thee!

Amen

This prayer was given by the Master in English.

PRAYER OF THE MISSION OF THE MASTER

Lord, our God, eternal rock and light of us all, may the harmony of Thy life embrace and enfold our souls.

We direct our souls towards Thee, Source of all goodness, Who gives life and health to Thy children and comforts them at all times.

Blessed art Thou, Lord, Who leads us on the path of Thy Light and blessest us through the Spirit of Thy boundless Mercy and limitless Love, through which Thy Glory is expressed.

We thank Thee for the beautiful life Thou hast given us, for all good things which Thou constantly doest for us, for all goods with which Thou showerest us and surroundest us and which come from Thee.

We thank Thee for our radiant thoughts and sublime feelings and noble influence which Thy Sacred Spirit gives us.

May the Light of Thy Wisdom illuminate the minds of all nations. May Thy Truth shine in every soul and may Thy Love flow through every heart so that the nations of the world enter into Love and know that life comes from Thee.

Do that which Thou hast said, that all will bow before Thee and will glorify Thy Name.

Support the leaders of the nations, so that they may accept the initiation of the Universal Brotherhood of Light and bring decisions into line with the Divine plan for brotherhood and unity among nations.

May the whole of heaven work with the Master and may his mission be crowned with success. May the Word of the Master enlighten every consciousness, may it be received and applied all over the world.

Awaken the spirit of the Bulgarian people, of the Slavs and of all nations which Thou hast called to fulfil his mission.

Support all his helpers, give them strength, knowledge, love and inspiration to work with joy for Thy Great Plan. Send even more workers into Thy Field.

Extend Thy Blessing upon us, who can do nothing without Thy Love and Benediction.

May we desire to live according to the law of Love, so as to be able through it to resolve the questions which stand before the door of our souls and to walk in Thy Sacred Path.

Send us each day Thy Peace and Thy Joy. Stretch forth Thy hands among us today. Thou hast always sustained us with Thy Love and we will serve Thee with our whole mind, with our whole heart and with our whole strength. From Thee we learn the great example of life.

May our life bear abundant fruit for the work of the Lord Jesus Christ and may we be a holy, living sacrifice, pleasing to Him. May the Holy Spirit of Christ inspire us in order to raise us and work through us.

Make us a chosen vessel of thy plan, support us to work for the coming of Thy Kingdom and its Justice on Earth. Teach us constantly to fulfil Thy Good Will and to glorify Thy Name with our life, according to Thy Love which accomplishes everything.

Amen

THE DIVINE PROMISE

A nd so, in everything you promise to Me, make sure that you tell them no falsehood, because you will be condemned to death. Know that you stand before me, your Lord, who knows your cunning and inconstant heart, which is full of all vices. That is why it must turn towards me and be renewed by My Spirit, cultivated and educated by My Word.

You, who will from now on become Mine and will entrust everything to My hands: from now on I alone will guide you; I alone will have your interests at heart and will arrange everything for you; I will teach you how to do everything. You will lie down and arise under My wing; you will dread Me and My eye will watch over the fate of your heart.

You will summon Me early in the morning and I will answer you with the early dawn. Before you call I will answer you and before you desire anything I will give you My Divine Gift.

I will watch over all your needs. See that you do not profane My Name nor stain My blessing.

Know that evil drives Me away and that I will protest against injustice and that I will be aggrieved by hard-heartedness.

After all this, always be ready to fulfil all My testament which I give you.

When you lie down, when you get up, when you eat, when you drink, whatever you are doing, you should thank God in your heart for everything.

I am the Lord who will confirm you in everything and your peace will rise like the morning Sun of Life.

Amen

PRAYER FOR THE EVENTS
composed during the Second World War

Lord of the strong, we Thy children turn towards Thee in these dreadful times which humanity is experiencing with the request to listen to the thrill and excitement of our souls.

The threat which is overhanging humanity on this planet and which might at any moment burst upon our heads is not hidden from us. To the east, battle and bloodshed, to the west battle and bloodshed. Human beings perish and no one thinks about their lives. Everyone considers his brother a deadly enemy and labours with all his might for his annihilation.

With this understanding it becomes dangerous to live in the world. The evil race has developed and wants to annihilate the whole of human culture which is the result of the efforts of Great Spirits who through the centuries have enlightened and directed humanity.

We know that this is the outcome of our past errors and that this is the liquidation of our errors, but do not compel us to pay all at once because we could scarcely find the strength to do so.

Lord, we ask Thee to put off the events, give us an extension with this liquidation, so that we may be able to bear what is coming more easily. Soften the impact, so that it becomes bearable.

Turn everything to the good!

May the neutrality of Bulgaria be established, so that Thy messenger may complete his mission undisturbed. Shorten the sufferings of humanity for the sake of the elect and establish peace in the world.

Hasten the awakening of consciousness so that Thy Kingdom may come to the world and that all people may direct their songs of praise towards Thy throne and for the greatness of Thy Name.

Bless, Lord, the Slavic element in the faces of the Bulgarian and Russian nations!

Amen

PRAYER – PRAISE TO THE LORD OF ALL AGES

Lord God, my soul quietly trusts in Thee. Thou hast revealed to us Thy path and we see Thy kindness, Thou hast shewn us Thy mercy and we see Thy long-suffering, Thou hast shewn us Thy Love and we see Thy goodness, Thou hast pointed us to the Truth and we see Thy Holiness.

Thou hast expressed Thy Name to us and we see Thy Justice, Thou hast revealed Thy Wisdom and we see Thy great deeds, Thou hast turned our hearts and we see Thy presence everywhere. Thou hast enlightened our minds and we see Thy creations, that all is good, Thou hast saved us with Thy strength and we know Thy might. And after all goods and blessings which Thou hast poured down upon us, according to Thine inner fullness, our desire is always to see Thy face and to rejoice in the fullness of Thy Love.

We thank Thee for Thy mercy and concern with which Thou hast surrounded us, we thank Thee that Thy mercy and kindness always follow us. We thank Thee that Thou always servest us, and art always ready to give us help and to support us when we are in need.

Kindly Lord, Holy Father of Heaven and Earth, deliver us from the wiles of the cunning one. Here Thou hast spoken to us, and we see that Thou wilt affirm us throughout all ages so as to glorify Thee.

Lord, our God, Who art changeless, sustain our weak brothers and sisters so that they may dwell in Thee and Thou mayest dwell in them, as Thou dwellest in me, so that we may all be one as Thou art with me, so that we may glorify Thee on earth with the fruits which we will bear in justice and mercy, so as to enlighten our deeds through people seeing us and glorifying Thee.

Kindly Father, Thou who givest us life and health, who provides us with bread and water and who makes us happy through the thousands of Thy blessings every day, Thy sun rises every morning like a newly-wed and runs its path which Thou hast ordained, bringing and sharing Thy blessings, which Thou hast bestowed on us. It brings and shares Thy blessings every day. In Thy Name it enlivens the whole earth and nature, brings the clouds, waters its face with rain and moisture, brings out every plant into the light, bestows all their beauty on the wild flowers, gladdens all animals and humans whom Thou hast made in Thy image, inspires hope and faith in their hearts for their work, while telling them that Thou wilt bless their labours.

How various and great are Thy laws. They cannot be numbered. We, Thy children, come today to bring Thee our gratitude, because Thou hast dressed us in the clothes of life. And how beautiful are these clothes in which Thou has dressed us.

Blessed Lord, blessed from all ages, receive now our grateful entreaty.

Amen

TESTAMENT OF THE MASTER

L ove the perfect path of Truth and Life.

Place goodness as the foundation of your house.

> Justice as its measure.
> Love as its adornment.
> Wisdom as its boundary
> Truth as its beacon

Only then will you know me and I will reveal myself to you.

BLESSING OF THE MASTER
BEINSA DOUNO

May Love be with you – it will bring you peace, joy and gratitude.

May the Love of the Holy Spirit shine within you.

> Be contented in the spirit.
> The sun of life is eternal radiance.

May my peace be with you all who dwell in divine purity.

May my Light and Love be always within you, disciples of life!

PSALMS

PSALM 117

Summons to praise

1 O praise the Lord all ye nations:
   praise him, all ye people.
2 For his merciful kindness is great towards us:
   and the truth of the Lord endureth for ever.
   Praise ye the Lord.

PSALM 91

God's protection

He that dwelleth in the secret place of the most High 1
    shall abide under the shadow of the Almighty.
I will say of the Lord, He is my refuge and my fortress: 2
    my God; in him will I trust.

Surely he shall deliver thee from the snare of the fowler, 3
    and from the noisome pestilence.
He shall cover thee with his feathers, 4
    and under his wings shalt thou trust:
    his truth shall be thy shield and buckler.

Thou shalt not be afraid for the terror by night; 5
    nor for the arrow that flieth by day;
Nor for the pestilence that walketh in darkness; 6
    nor for the destruction that wasteth at noonday.

A thousand shall fall at thy side, 7
    and ten thousand at the right hand;
    but it shall not come nigh thee.
Only with thine eyes shalt thou behold and see 8
    the reward of the wicked.

Because thou hast made the Lord, which is thy refuge, 9
    even the most High, thy habitation.
There shall no evil befall thee, neither shall any plague 10
    come near thy dwelling.

11 For he shall give his angels charge over thee,
   to keep thee in all thy ways.
12 They shall bear thee up in their hands,
   lest thou dash thy foot against a stone.

13 Thou shalt tread upon the lion and the adder:
   the young lion and the dragon
   shalt thou trample under feet.
14 Because he hath set his love upon me,
   therefore will I deliver him:
   I will set him on high
   because he hath known my name.

15 He shall call upon me, and I will answer him:
   I will be with him in trouble;
   I will deliver him and honour him.
16 With long life will I satisfy him,
   and shew him my salvation.

PSALM 133

Brotherly love

Behold how good and how pleasant it is for brethren   1
to dwell together in unity.
It is like the precious ointment on the head,
that ran down upon the beard, even Aaron's beard: 2
that went down to the skirts of his garments;
As the dew of Hermon, and as the dew that descended   3
upon the mountains of Zion:
for there the Lord commanded the blessing,
even life for evermore.

PSALM 23

The Good Shepherd

1 The Lord is my shepherd; I shall not want

2 He maketh me to lie down in green pastures;
he leadeth me beside the still waters.

3 He restoreth my soul:
he leadeth me in the paths of righteousness
for his name's sake.

4 Yea, though I walk through the valley of the shadow of
death, I will fear no evil: for thou art with me; thy
rod and thy staff they comfort me.

5 Thou preparest a table before me
in the presence of mine enemies:
thou anointest my head with oil;
my cup runneth over.

6 Surely goodness and mercy shall follow me
all the days of my life:
and I will dwell in the house of the Lord for ever.

PSALM 121

A guardian of Israel

I will lift up mine eyes unto the hills,   1
  from whence cometh my help.
My help cometh from the Lord,   2
    which made heaven and earth.

He will not suffer thy foot to be moved: 3
    he that keepeth thee will not slumber.
Behold, he that keepeth Israel   4
    shall neither slumber nor sleep.

The Lord is thy keeper:the Lord is thy shade upon thy   5
    right hand.
The sun shall not smite thee by day,nor the moon by   6
    night.

The Lord shall preserve thee from all evil: 7
    he shall preserve thy soul.
The Lord shall preserve thy going out and thy coming in   8
    from this time forth and even for evermore.

PSALM 61 – SUNDAY

Prayer of an exile

1 Hear my cry, O God; attend unto my prayer.

2 From the end of the earth I will cry unto thee,
    when my heart is overwhelmed:
      lead me to the rock that is higher than me.

3 For thou hast been a shelter for me,
    and a strong tower from the enemy.

4 I will abide in thy tabernacle for ever:
    I will trust in the covert of thy wings. Shelah.

5 For thou, O God, hast heard my vows:
    thou hast given me the heritage of those
      that fear thy name.

6 Thou wilt prolong the king's life:
    and his years as many generations.

7 He shall abide before God for ever:
    O prepare mercy and truth,
      which may preserve him.

8 So will I sing praise unto thy name for ever,
    that I may daily perform my vows.

PSALM 143 – MONDAY

A humble entreaty

H ear my prayer, O Lord,   1
  give ear to my supplications:
    in thy faithfulness answer me,
    and in thy righteousness.
And enter not into judgment with thy servant: 2
    for in thy sight shall no man living be justified.

For the enemy hath persecuted my soul;   3
    he hath smitten my life down to the ground;
    he hath made me to dwell in darkness,
    as those that have been long dead.
Therefore is my spirit overwhelmed within me;   4
    my heart within me is desolate.

I remember the days of old;   5
    I meditate on all thy works;
    I muse on the work of thy hands.
I stretch forth my hands unto thee: 6
    my soul thirsteth after thee,
    as a thirsty land. Shelah.

7 Hear me speedily, O Lord: my spirit faileth:
    hide not thy face from me,
      lest I be like unto them that go down into the pit.

8 Cause me to hear thy loving-kindness in the morning;
    for in thee do I trust:
    cause me to know the way wherein I should walk;
    for I lift up my soul unto thee.

9 Deliver me, O Lord, from mine enemies;
    I flee unto thee to hide me.

10 Teach me to do thy will;
    for thou art my God: thy spirit is good;
    lead me into the land of uprightness.

11 Quicken me, O Lord, for thy name's sake:
    for thy righteousness' sake
    bring my soul out of trouble.

12 And of thy mercy cut off mine enemies,
    and destroy all them that afflict my soul:
    for I am thy servant.

PSALM 27 – TUESDAY

In God's company there is no fear

The Lord is my light and my salvation; 1
whom shall I fear?
The Lord is the strength of my life;
of whom shall I be afraid?

When the wicked, even mine enemies and my foes, 2
came upon me to eat up my flesh,
they stumbled and fell.

Though an host should encamp against me, 3
my heart shall not fear:
though war should rise up against me,
in this will I be confident.
One thing have I desired of the Lord, 4
that I will seek after;
that I may dwell in the house of the Lord
all the days of my life,
to behold the beauty of the Lord,
and to enquire in his temple.

For in the time of trouble 5
he shall hide me in his pavilion:
in the secret of his tabernacle shall he hide me;
he shall set me up upon a rock.

6 And now shall mine head be lifted up
    above mine enemies round about me:
    therefore will I offer in his tabernacle sacrifices of joy;
    I will sing, yea, I will sing praises unto the Lord.

7 Hear me, O Lord, when I cry with my voice:
    have mercy also upon me, and answer me.
8 When thou saidst, Seek ye my face;
    my heart said unto thee,
    thy face, O Lord, will I seek.

9 Hide not thy face far from me;
    put not thy servant away in anger:
    thou hast been my help; leave me not,
    neither forsake me, O God of my salvation.
10 When my father and my mother forsake me,
    then the Lord will take me up.

11 Teach me thy way, O Lord,
    and lead me in a plain path,
    because of mine enemies.
12 Deliver me not over unto the will of mine enemies:
    for false witnesses are risen up against me,
    and such as breathe out cruelty.

13 I had fainted, unless I had believed to see
    the goodness of the Lord in the land of the living.

14 Wait on the Lord: be of good courage,
    and he shall strengthen thine heart:
    wait, I say, on the Lord.

PSALM 19 – WEDNESDAY

Yahweh, the sun of righteousness

The heavens declare the glory of God;   1
    and the firmament sheweth his handiwork.
Day unto day uttereth speech,   2
    and night unto night sheweth knowledge.

There is no speech nor language,   3
    where their voice is not heard.
Their line is gone out through all the earth,   4
    and their words to the end of the world.
    In them hath he set a tabernacle for the sun.

Which is a bridegroom coming out of his chamber,   5
    and rejoiceth as the strong man to run a race.
His going forth from the end of heaven,   6
    and his circuits unto the ends of it:
    and there is nothing hid from the heat thereof.

The law of the Lord is perfect, converting the soul: 7
    the testimony of the Lord is sure,
    making wise the simple.
The statutes of the Lord are right, rejoicing the heart: 8
    the commandment of the Lord is pure,
    enlightening the eyes.

9 The fear of the Lord is clean, enduring for ever:
　　the judgments of the lord are true
　　and righteous altogether.
10 More to be desired are they than gold,
　　yea than much fine gold:
　　sweeter also than honey and the honeycomb.

11 Moreover by them is thy servant warned:
　　and keeping of them there is great reward.
12 Who can understand his errors?
　　Cleanse thou me from secret faults.

13 Keep back thy servant also from presumptuous sins;
　　let them not have dominion over me:
　　then shall I be upright,
　　and I shall be innocent from the great transgression.

14 Let the words of my mouth
　　and the meditation of my heart,
　　be acceptable in thy sight,
　　O Lord, my strength and my redeemer.

PSALM 103 – WEDNESDAY

God is love

Bless the Lord, O my soul: 1
and all that is within me, bless his holy name.
Bless the Lord, O my soul,   2
and forget not all his benefits.

Who forgiveth all thine iniquities;   3
who healeth all thy diseases;
Who redeemeth thy life from destruction;   4
who crowneth thee with loving-kindness
and tender mercies;

Who satisfieth thy mouth with good things;   5
so that thy youth is renewed like the eagle's.
The Lord executeth righteousness and judgment   6
for all that are oppressed.

He made known his ways unto Moses,   7
his acts unto the children of Israel.
The Lord is merciful and slow to anger,   8
and plenteous in his mercy.

He will not always chide;   9
neither will he keep his anger for ever.
He hath not dealt with us after our sins;   10
nor rewarded us according to our iniquities.

For as the heaven is high above the earth,   11
so great is his mercy toward them that fear him.

12 As far as the east is from the west,
    so far hath he removed our transgressions from us.

13 Like as a father pitieth his children,
    so the Lord pitieth them that fear him.
14 For he knoweth our frame;
    he remembereth that we are dust.

15 As for man, his days are as grass:
    as a flower of the field, so he flourisheth.
16 For the wind passeth over it and it is gone;
    and the place thereof shall know it no more.

17 But the mercy of the Lord
    is from everlasting to everlasting
    upon them that fear him,
    and his righteousness unto his children's children;
18 To such as keep his covenant,
    and to those that remember
    his commandments to do them.

19 The Lord hath prepared his throne in the heavens;
    and his kingdom ruleth over all.
20 Bless the Lord, ye his angels, that excel in strength,
    that do his commandments,
    hearkening unto the voice of his word.

21 Bless ye the Lord, all ye his hosts;
    ye ministers of his, that do his pleasure.
22 Bless the Lord, all his works in all places of his dominion;
    bless the Lord, O my soul.

PSALM 112 – THURSDAY

In praise of the virtuous

Praise ye the Lord.   1
  Blessed is the man that feareth the Lord,
    that delighteth greatly in his commandments.
His seed shall be mighty upon earth: 2
    the generation of the upright shall be blessed.

Wealth and riches shall be in his house: 3
    and his righteousness endureth for ever.
Unto the upright there ariseth light in darkness: 4
    he is gracious, and full of compassion, and righteous.

A good man sheweth favour, and lendeth: 5
    he will guide his affairs with discretion.
Surely he shall not be moved for ever: 6
    the righteous shall be in everlasting remembrance.

He shall not be afraid of evil tidings: 7
    his heart is fixed, trusting in the Lord.
His heart is established, he shall not be afraid,   8
    until he see his desire upon his enemies.

He hath dispersed, he hath given to the poor;   9
    His righteousness endureth for ever;
    his horn shall be exalted with honour.

The wicked shall see it and be grieved;   10
    he shall gnash with his teeth, and melt away:
    the desire of the wicked shall perish.

PSALM 44 – FRIDAY

National lament

1 We have heard with our ears, O God,
   our fathers have told us,
    what work thou didst in their days,
    in the times of old.
2 How thou didst drive out the heathen with thy hand,
    and plantedst them;
    how thou didst afflict the people, and cast them out.

3 For they got not the land in their possession
    by their own sword,
    neither did their own arm save them:
    but thy right hand, and thine arm,
    and the light of thy countenance,
    because thou hadst a favour unto them.
4 Thou art my King, O God:
    command deliverances for Jacob.

5 Through thee will we push down our enemies:
    through thy name will we tread them
    that rise up against us.
6 For I will not trust in my bow,
    neither shall my sword save me.

7 But thou hast saved us from our enemies,
    and hast put them to shame that hated us.
8 In God we boast all the day long,
    and praise thy name for ever. Shelah.

But thou hast cast off, and put us to shame;   9
   and goest not forth with our armies.

Thou makest us to turn back from the enemy: 10
   and they which hate us spoil for themselves.

Thou hast given us like sheep appointed for meat: 11
   and hast scattered us among the heathen.
Thou sellest thy people for nought,   12
   and dost not increase thy wealth by their price.

Thou makest us a reproach to our neighbours,   13
   a scorn and a derision
   to them that are round about us.
Thou makest us a byword among the heathen,   14
   a shaking of the head among the people.

My confusion is continually before me,   15
   and the shame of my face hath covered me,
For the voice of him that reproacheth and blasphemeth;   16
   by reason of the enemy and avenger.

All this is come upon us; yet we have not forgotten thee,   17
   neither have we dealt falsely with thy covenant.
Our heart is not turned back,   18
   neither have our steps declined from thy way;

Though thou hast sore broken us in the place of the   19
   dragons,and covered us with the shadow of death.
If we have forgotten the name of our God,   20
   or stretched out our hands to a strange god;

21 Shall not God search this out?
    for he knoweth the secrets of the heart.
22 Yea, for thy sake are we killed all day long;
    we are counted as sheep for the slaughter.

23 Awake, why sleepest thou, O Lord?
    arise, cast us not off for ever.
24 Wherefore hidest thou thy face,
    and forgettest our affliction and oppression?

25 For our soul is bowed down in the dust:
    our belly cleaveth to the earth.
26 Arise for our help, and redeem us for thy mercies' sake.

PSALM 25 – SATURDAY

Prayer in danger

Unto thee O Lord do I lift up my soul.   1

O my God, I trust in thee: let me not be ashamed,   2
   let not mine enemies triumph over me.

Yea, let none that wait on thee be ashamed: 3
   let them be ashamed which transgress without cause.
Shew me thy ways, O Lord; teach me thy paths.   4

Lead me in thy truth, and teach me: 5
   for thou art the God of my salvation;
   on thee do I wait all day.
Remember, O Lord, thy tender mercies   6
   and thy loving-kindnesses;
   for they have been ever of old.

Remember not the sins of my youth,   7
   nor my transgressions:
   according to thy mercy remember thou me
   for thy goodness' sake, O Lord.
Good and upright is the Lord: 8
   therefore will he teach sinners in the way.

The meek will he guide in judgment: 9
   and the meek will he teach his way.
All the paths of the Lord are mercy and truth   10
   unto such as keep his covenant and his testimonies.

11 For thy name's sake O Lord, pardon mine iniquity;
      for it is great.
12 What man is he that feareth the Lord:
      him shall he teach in the way that he shall choose.

13 His soul shall dwell at ease;
      and his seed shall inherit the earth.
14 The secret of the Lord is with them that fear him;
      and he will shew them his covenant.

15 Mine eyes are ever toward the Lord;
      for he shall pluck my feet out of the net.
16 Turn thee unto me, and have mercy upon me;
      for I am desolate and afflicted.

17 The troubles of my heart are enlarged:
      O bring thou me out of my distresses.
18 Look upon mine affliction and my pain:
      and forgive all my sins.

19 Consider mine enemies; for they are many;
      and they hate me with cruel hatred.
20 O keep my soul, and deliver me: let me not be ashamed;
      for I put my trust in thee.

21 Let integrity and uprightness preserve me;
      for I wait on thee.
22 Redeem Israel, O God,
      out of all his troubles.

FORMULAS

Note: These formulas are condensed types of prayer affirmations which are used either as invocations or in specific situations as suggested below. Many of these formulas are repeated three times, as indicated: once for the Divine world, once for the spiritual world and once for the physical world.

The disciple must have:
    A heart as pure as a crystal,
    A mind as bright as the sun,
    A soul as vast as the universe,
    A spirit as powerful as God and
    one with God.

(three times)

May we be
    As pure as light,
    As transparent as water,
    As abundant as love,
    As radiant as truth,
    As harmonious as wisdom,
    As firm and unshakeable as justice,
    As stable as virtue.

May my thoughts be as radiant as the sun;
    May my feelings be as pure as the water
    from mountain springs!

May God be glorified in the Brotherhood of Light, and
    may the Brothers be glorified in the Love of God.

(three times)

*(This was one of the last formulas given by the Master and is
used at the end of the prayers.)*

Be always faithful, true, pure and kind, and the God of
    Peace will fill your heart with all goodness.

(three times)

Lord, our God, may Thy Kingdom come on earth, as it is
    in Heaven, and may all nations whom Thou hast called
    take their place in Thy Kingdom, in order to serve Thee
    with joy and gladness.

(three times)

God reigns in Heaven, God reigns on earth,
    Blessed be his name.

(three times)

Only the luminous path of Wisdom leads to Truth.
    Life is hidden in Truth.

(three times)

May the peace of God and the blessing of God
    Encompass and enfold the whole earth.

(three times)

The Love of God brings fullness of life,
    The Wisdom of God brings fullness of light,
    The Truth of God brings perfect freedom!
    Great is God in Love!
    Great is God in Wisdom!
    Great is God in Truth!
    In Love God instructs.
    In Wisdom God enlightens.
    In Truth God liberates.
    Merciful and compassionate is the Lord
    And His Kindness is above all things.
    His exaltation sustains everything.
    Everything lives and moves in the Lord.
    He is gladness and joy in all that lives in the world.

Lord, we wish to receive the Spirit of Love

(three times)

Lord, we wish to receive the Spirit of Wisdom

(three times)

Lord, we wish to receive the Spirit of Truth

(three times)

Blessed be Thy Name, Lord, now and for ever.

Lord, may Thy Spirit of Love, Thy Spirit of Wisdom, Thy
    Spirit of Truth arise in our hearts.

God is Love
    God is All-Wise
    God is Gentle

(three times)

Great art Thou, O Lord.
  Great are Thy deeds.
  Great is Thy Name above all.
  I send my Love towards Thee.
  I see Thee and love Thee in everything and everyone.

Merciful, holy and kind Lord, show me the light of Thy
  face so that I may do Thy Will.

For Thy sake, Lord, who liveth in my soul from all
  eternity, I wish to learn and serve Thee.

Lord, I wish with my whole heart, with my whole mind,
  with my whole soul and strength to fulfil Thy Good
  Will, without any exception.

Lord, with the strength of Thy Love and Wisdom, may the
  Virtues which Thou hast planted in my soul from the
  beginning grow within me; I will apply my whole
  strength towards the fulfilment of Thy Will.

God has placed everything in my soul. I wish to fulfil the
  Will of God, to fulfil the Divine Plan, whatever God
  has intended for me. May the Will of God be done. I
  will work as God has ordained.

With the Power of Thy Love, I wish, Lord, that the virtues
  which Thou hast planted within my soul from the
  beginning should grow. And I will apply all my strength
  towards the fulfilment of Thy Will.

Lord, may the Divine which Thou hast deposited in my
    soul grow within me.

Lord, our God, may Thy Kingdom come on earth, as it is
    in heaven, and may all nations which Thou hast
    summoned take their place in Thy Kingdom, so as to
    serve Thee with joy and gladness.

(three times)

God is Spirit and whoever serves Him must serve Him in
    Spirit and in Truth!
    God is Love and whoever knows Him must serve Him
    in Spirit and in Truth!

Lord, may everything be for Thy Glory and for the Good
    of my soul.
(Formula given by the Master to be said after prayer)

May we be ready to receive the word of God in our minds,
    in our hearts and in our souls and then to apply it.
    Amen, so be it.

(three times)

Lord, I thank Thee thousands and millions of times.
*(This formula is very important; it has a magical strength. When
things get really bad, pronounce this formula within yourself and
see what happens within your soul. Only say this formula when
you are not thinking anything bad. And when you say it, your
path will always open up everywhere and it is the most natural
means to deal with your difficulties and you will achieve everything for which you were born. Say three times.)*

In the fulfilment of the Will of God lies the power of the
    human soul.

(three times)

In the Divine plan I am to grow in virtue.
    In the Divine plan I am to mature in Divine justice.
    In the Divine plan I am to live in Divine Truth.
    In the Divine plan I am to blossom in Divine Wisdom.
    In the Divine plan I am to ripen in Divine Love.
    Therefore I am on the path of Truth and Divine life. So
    no one can take this right away from me. This is my
    own right. Where God is, there am I also.

My heart is warm, my soul is fresh, my mind is bright, my
    spirit is strong, because I live in the law of infinite,
    changeless Love.

Lord, may Thy Love, Thy Wisdom, Thy Truth, Thy
    Justice and Thy Goodness dwell within me.

The faith in which I live will bring Divine harmony into
    the strivings of my heart.

Ever kindly Father of all fullness, in the Name of Thy
    Love, illuminate me with Thy kind Spirit and fill my
    heart with Thy peace.

May we sanctify the Name of God.
    May we seek the Kingdom of God and His
    Righteousness.
    May we fulfil the Will of God.
(The Master often pronounced this formula in the school in

front of the disciples)

God is Love. If you love Me, you will keep my
  commandments. I and my Father will come and make a
  dwelling in you and I will manifest Myself to you.

May the peace of God abide, and may Divine joy and
  Divine exaltation shine in our hearts.

(three times)

There is no love like the Love of God;
  Only the Love of God is Love.
  There is no wisdom like the Wisdom of God;
  Only the Wisdom of God is Wisdom.
  There is no truth like the Truth of God;
  Only the Truth of God is Truth.
  There is no justice like the Justice of God;
  Only the Justice of God is Justice.
  There is no virtue like the Virtue of God;
  Only the Virtue of God is Virtue.
  There is no power like the Power of the Spirit,
  Only the Power of the Spirit is the Power of God.

When you visit a house:
  Lord, send Thy blessing upon this house.

When a guest comes to you:
  Lord, I thank Thee for Thy visit through this person.

FORMULAS WHEN IN DIFFICULTY

Lord, Thou art the One who can set everything right.
   Thou wilt arrange things for the best.

Amen

However difficult this work, I will finish it with God and
   with the Spirit which guides me.
*(The Master recommended the use of this formula when you
find yourself in great difficulties. He called it the priceless formula)*

Lord, I am weak, Thou art strong, May Thy strength be
   manifest!
*(Important formula of the Master to be used when you
encounter problems)*

Lord, all things are possible for Thee. Thy Spirit, which
   Thou hast sent to guide us, can do everything through
   Thee. And we can do everything through Thy Spirit.

As soon as you encounter a contradiction, you may say:
For God, everything is possible.
   I live in God and with His Wisdom I can achieve
   everything.

You may say to your soul:
God is with you, you will prevail, your victory is my
   victory. I believe only in one God of Wisdom and in
   one Spirit of Truth.

Without fear and without darkness.
Without fear in boundless Love.

God of Love is not the God of the dead but the God of the living. I am alive and this God is within me, and since He is my God, with Him I can do everything.

FORMULAS FOR PROTECTION

In the Name of Divine Love,
In the Name of Divine Wisdom,
In the Name of Divine Truth,
in which I live and move and have my being, and with the power of the living Word of God, may all evil and cunning thoughts and all hostile powers be dispersed.
(three times)

God of Love, God of Light, disperse all impure influences around me.

Guard me, Lord, with Thy sacred Name through all the days of our life. We commend our Spirit into Thy hands. Guide us with the lights of Thy teaching.

I acknowledge only One Spirit of Truth and I call upon the Power of that Spirit to enfold me.

God is Love, God is Wisdom, I am goodness, I am Truth
Note: If evil comes to you, do not attack it, but simply defend

yourself. If any temptation comes your way, quietly say to your-self: 'God is Love, God is Wisdom, I am goodness, I am Truth'. This formula is a strong weapon against evil. Make way for God within yourself and manifest His Love and Wisdom. Say three times.

MORNING

Lord, I thank Thee for everything Thou hast given me and taught me. (In the morning on getting out of bed.)

Lord, I thank Thee that I have risen, I thank Thee that I am alive. Tell me what I can do for Thee today.

Lord, give me Strength, Life and Health to work for Thy Great Plan.

Love, study, keep silent, endure, forgive, pursue your path and do not forget God!

Always be glad. Pray without ceasing. Give thanks for everything. Do not extinguish the spirit.

Place the Truth in your soul and you will acquire the freedom which you seek.
Place wisdom in your mind, light will come and knowledge will give you its aid.
Place purity in your heart, Love will come and the true life will begin.

O great Love, the beginning of every goodness in our life,
as Thy child, support me in the acquisition of
knowledge. I feel my link with Thee, and in my striving
towards Thee I am not afraid of worldly temptation and
I believe that I will fulfil my purpose in uniting with
Thee.

Amen

I must think like God, I must love as He loves.

May the Kingdom of God come on earth and may I be a
bearer of His Light.

(three times)

God is Love, Love which Christ has received;
Christ is Love, Love which we have received;
We are Love, Love which we are now manifesting.
Blessed be the Lord.

(three times)

Christ is the man of the fullness of strength.
Christ is the man of the fullness of faith.
Christ is the man of the fullness of love.

(three times)

EVENING

Lord, surround me with Thy light and protect me during
the time of my nightly rest. I am going to study, to pray
and to work.

Lord of the Strong, send Thy Sacred Spirit of Strength to
illuminate my room with Thy strength and the Powers
of Thy Spirit, surround my bed with the fiery circle of
Thy Love so that my room and my whole house may be
freed from evil influences.

Lord, may Thy Peace and Thy Joy abide with us always so
that our hearts may be illuminated and that we may
serve Thee with our whole heart, with our whole mind,
with our whole soul and with our whole strength.

Lord, I ask Thee to send me an angel to teach me how to
do the smallest good, to teach me to do the smallest act
of love, to teach me the smallest knowledge, to teach me
to give people the smallest freedom and how to manifest
the smallest mercy.

The perfecting of Love will be the meaning of my life.
Perfect Love casts out every fear from the soul and
brings peace and gladness to the spirit.

I shall lie down in peace and sleep, because only Thou,
Lord, makest me live in safety.

I know one God of Love, one Teacher of Wisdom and one
Spirit of Truth, which we call upon to come with its
life-giving strength to disperse all evil influences

(three times)

Lord, I thank Thee that Thou hast given me an excellent
mind in which Thou hast placed Thy Wisdom, and
excellent heart in which Thou hast placed Thy Love. I
wish to serve Thee with this Love and Wisdom.

Lord, may Thy Peace and Thy Joy be always with us, so
that our hearts may be illuminated and that we may
serve Thee with our whole heart, with our whole mind,
with our whole soul and with our whole strength.

For the sake of Thee, Lord, Whom I have carried in my
soul from eternity, I will listen to Thee and serve Thee.

God is Light. The angels are warmth.
People are kindness.

(three times)

God is light within me.
My spirit is warmth.
I am kindness.

(three times)

When you begin to hear a thundering, when the earth begins to shake beneath your feet, say to yourself the following:
Everything which is good, I may receive; everything which is good, I may apply. Whenever I wish to do any kind of good, there is no power which can prevent me. I can do everything through the living Lord of Love, who has created everything in the world.

May this thought remain with you in all events of your life, and do not fear.

FORMULA BEFORE AND AFTER EATING

The Love of God brings abundance and fullness of life.
Only the Love of God brings abundance and fullness of life.
Only the manifestation of the Love of God brings abundance and fullness of life.
Note: Only the first part of the formula is usually used – repeat three times.

FOR HEALING

Lord, Thou art the source of life, send us Thy life-giving strength, Thy Spirit to heal us from all illnesses and sufferings.

(three times)

And this is eternal life: to know Thee, the One True God
  and Christ whom Thou sent.
  And this is eternal life: to know Love, Wisdom and
  Truth.
  And this is eternal life: to know that God is Spirit which
  reigns everywhere.

Love is coming.

(three times)

I am mobilised, I have work, I serve God. And therefore
  may all spirits which cause illnesses go away.

I strip off the old person of toil.
  I strip off all my my infirmities, illnesses and errors, and
  send them into the world.
  I put on the new person of Love, Wisdom and Truth,
  Justice and Virtue.

(three times)

I live in God and God lives in me. And in God there is no
  illness at all. So I must be healthy and I am healthy.

I have inexhaustible wealth at my disposal. I live in the
  fullness of Divine Love, I breathe the light of Divine
  Wisdom, I move in the great Divine Truth, which
  brings freedom and scope to souls, arousing everything
  which God gives me.

I wish my heart to become rhythmical, to merge with the
pulse of the sun and to send its energy to the whole
organism, just as the sun sends its energy to the whole
world.

I am ready to serve God. I am serving God. I work for
God. So I must be healthy. And I am healthy.

*For good health, the Master recommended that one read at
7.00 in the evening:*
1. The Good Prayer
2. Psalm 91
3. The Path of Life
4. The Prayer of the Elect
5. 'We pray to the Lord Jesus Christ' (three times)
6. Our Father

Pronounce the following formula when sunbathing:
Lord, I thank Thee for the sacred energy of Divine life
which Thou sendest us with the sun's rays. I feel
intensely how it penetrates into all my organs bringing
strength, life and health to my whole body. It is the
reflection of Thy Love towards us. I thank Thee. Lord,
Thou art strong and almighty. If it is Thy wish, Thou
canst free this person from his sufferings.

Motto
Thou, O Supreme, who blessest and createst, set right
everything in me and around me. Come, rectify my
mind, may it think rightly. Come, rectify my heart, may
living love well up in it.

Formulas for breathing
(for the absorption of electromagnetic energy (prana) with deep breathing.

Breathing in:
I thank Thee, Lord, for the Divine life which Thou hast placed in the air and which I receive together with it.

Holding breath:
This Divine life permeates my whole body and brings strength, life and health to every part.

Breathing out:
May this Divine life manifest outwardly through my actions.

For the absorption of Divine Love, Wisdom and Truth:

Breathing in:
May the Name of God be glorified within me.

Holding breath:
May the Kingdom of God and His Justice come within me.

Breathing out:
May the Will of God be done

These are done first through the left, then through the right nostril.

WEEKLY ROUTINE

Every day: Psalm 91, Psalm 23, the Lord's Prayer

Sunday
1. In the Beginning was the Word (song)
2. The Good Prayer
3. Psalm 61

Monday
1. Bless the Lord, my Soul (song)
2. The Prayer of the Kingdom
3. Psalm 143

Tuesday
1. I will Rejoice (song)
2. The Path of Life
3. Psalm 27

Wednesday
1. The Song of the Sacred Path
2. The Prayer of the Kingdom
3. Psalms 19, 103

Thursday
1. He is Coming (song)
2. The Fruits of the Spirit
3. Psalm 112

Friday
1. Fir-Fur-Fen (song)
2. Prayer of the Triune God
3. Psalm 44

Saturday
1. God is Love
2. The Small Prayer
3. Psalm 25